Theory and Interpretation of Narrative

James Phelan and Peter J. Rabinowitz, Series Editors

Unnatural Voices

Extreme Narration in Modern and Contemporary Fiction

BRIAN RICHARDSON

THE OHIO STATE UNIVERSITY PRESS / COLUMBUS

Library of Congress Cataloging-in-Publication Data
Richardson, Brian, 1953–
Unnatural voices: extreme narration in modern and contemporary fiction / Brian Richardson.
p. cm.—(Theory and interpretation of narrative)
Includes bibliographical references and index.
ISBN-13: 978-0-8142-1041-3 (cloth : alk. paper)
ISBN-13: 978-0-8142-5157-7 (pbk. : alk. paper)
ISBN-13: 978-0-8142-9119-1 (cd-rom)
1. Fiction—Technique. 2. Narration (Rhetoric) 3. Fiction—20th century—History and criticism. 4. Fiction—19th century—History and criticism. I. Title. II. Series: Theory and interpretation of narrative series.
PN3383.N35R53 2006
809.3'83—dc22
2006017229

Cover photo and cover design by Jason Moore.
Text design and typesetting by Jennifer Shoffey Forsythe.
Type set in Sabon.
Printed by Thomson-Shore, Inc.

The paper used in this publication meets the minimum requirements of the American National Standard for Information Sciences—Permanence of Paper for Printed Library Materials. ANSI Z39.48-1992.

9 8 7 6 5 4 3 2 1

To my brother, Alan

Extraordinary reader, intimate friend, and great
companion, who many years ago joined me on a beach in Mexico
where we first read Joyce and Proust

contents

preface

Narrative theory, despite its emphasis on narration and narrators, has not yet systematically examined the impressive range of unusual postmodern and other avant garde strategies of narration. At the same time, though postmodernism is certainly the most important and successful literary movement of the last half century, it is one that has often proven resistant to traditional narrative theory. This book is intended to rectify these unfortunate absences. It explores in depth one of the most significant aspects of late modernist, avant garde, and postmodern narrative—the creation, fragmentation, and reconstitution of narrative voices—and offers a theoretical account of these unusual and innovative strategies. This is an empirical study that describes and theorizes the actual practices of significant authors, instead of building on *a priori* linguistic or rhetorical categories; such an inductive approach is essential because many extreme forms of narration seem to have been invented precisely to transgress fundamental linguistic and rhetorical categories. By drawing on a wide range of examples and utilizing the work of postmodern narrative theorists, I hope to give these practices the thorough analysis they deserve. I will also take care to identify substantial if unexpected antecedents in earlier texts by authors ranging from Gogol to Conrad as well as apposite modern and contemporary works not usually considered from this perspective. In addition, I include some discussion of the work of Samuel Beckett in each chapter, thus providing a single (if knotty) thread that runs throughout the book.

The *first* chapter, "Transgressing Self and Voice," begins with a brief inventory of a number of innovative contemporary uses of narrators and narration, including narration by animals, small children, corpses, machines, and a Minotaur, which move ever further away from conventional human speakers. We will look briefly at the career of Robbe-Grillet, and follow out the varied construction and deconstruction of the narrators of his fictions. The chapter goes on to provide a theoretical overview of recent deployments of narration and describes a new kind of textual drama that hinges on the disclosure of the unexpected identity of the narrator at the end of the work. The chapter outlines the existing range of first, second, and third person forms, including such unusual types as "it," "they," and passive voice narration. I then contrast these practices with current theories of narrative poetics which are unable to fully comprehend the distinctive difference of such work. While concentrating on postmodern works, I also pay attention to earlier and adjacent forms, noting salient continuities and ruptures.

The *second* chapter studies second person narration in depth, identifying three major forms of second person fiction, reflecting on its functions and nature, and commenting on the reasons for its utilization by authors from a number of minority or disenfranchised communities. The *third* chapter traces the development of fiction narrated in the first person plural from its unexpected origins in Conrad's *Nigger of the 'Narcissus'* to its more familiar present incarnations and its less known postcolonial avatars. This chapter elucidates the play of unreliability, the knowledge of other minds, and the constitution of a collective subject in these texts. I also discuss "we" narration as a vehicle for representations of intersubjective feminist, agrarian, revolutionary, and postcolonial consciousnesses. The *fourth* chapter surveys recent developments in multiperson narration, that is, texts that employ both first and third or, in some cases, first, second, and third person narration. It also discusses indeterminate speakers and logically impossible acts of narration. It assesses claims and debates that stretch from Lukács to feminism and new historicism concerning the ideological valence of specific kinds of narration. Having completed three chapters of analysis of the most prominent alternative forms of narration, I then go on to offer a flexible model that can situate all of these odd but increasingly common voices.

These analyses in turn are followed by explorations of new areas of experimental narration that have not been studied from the vantage point of a comprehensive approach to the theory of narration. I begin (in Chapter *Five*) with an examination of three curious narrating figures that exist at the limits of the utterable: The first is what I call the "interlocutor," or the voice that asks questions that the rest of the narrative then answers. This feature, found in the catechistic chapter ("Ithaca") in Joyce's *Ulysses,* is fairly common in postmodern fiction, and occupies an unusual and unstable position between narrator and narratee. The second is the phenomenon of "denarration," voices that erase the texts that they have been creating, such as found in the sentences, "Yesterday it was raining. Yesterday it was not raining." The last, which I call the "permeable narrator," slips (or is collapsed) into other minds and discourses and speaks what should be impossible for it to know; this is a favorite strategy of Beckett, especially in the trilogy, and is common in subsequent French fiction and elsewhere. I conclude this chapter with a brief analysis of distinctively postmodern types of unreliability. Chapter *Six* surveys unusual narrators and anti-mimetic kinds of narration in contemporary drama, focusing on the more outrageous practices of Stoppard, Duras, David Henry Hwang, Paula Vogel, and (naturally) Beckett. I focus on plays in which the nature and identity of the narrator constitutes part of the drama of the work, where offstage voices construct events, and the contents of one mind contaminates another.

The *seventh* chapter reassesses the question of the implied author and argues for the continued viability of this concept by assembling a range of texts that have two or more historical authors and either one or more implied authors. I also examine works by a single author that seem to emerge from antithetical aesthetic stances and speculate on the implications of such texts for a theory of the implied author. I discuss the limits and utility of the concept, and point to places where the author's voice seems to override that of the narrator. Booth's concept of the "career implied author" is reassessed and found relevant for the analysis of the larger oeuvre of writers throughout the history of fiction. I go on to take up the understudied topic of multiple implied readers in a work and compare it to the case of multiple implied authors of a single text. I conclude with a new model of the narrator–implied author–historical author continuum.

In the final chapter, I summarize the main argument of the book and go on to discuss further the modernist origins and historical antecedents of the anti-realist practices of so many contemporary works. Finally, I end with a description of a general "anti-poetics" of narrative for these and other anti-representational works to be conceived as a supplement and foil to the traditional poetics based on mimetic and "natural" narratives. I advocate the move away from rigid typologies and Chinese box-type models of embedded speakers and toward an alternate figuration that stresses the permeability, instability, and playful mutability of the voices of nonmimetic fictions. It is hoped that this book will fill a large gap in narrative theory, contribute to scholarship on Samuel Beckett and on modern and postmodern fiction, and help provide enhanced coverage, precision, and conceptual modeling for the theory and analysis of narrators and narration.

acknowledgments

This book has benefited greatly from the generous comments of many colleagues. I am especially thankful to Monika Fludernik, William Nelles, and Porter Abbott, who read and commented on most or all of the chapters. Deep thanks also to those who read and commented on individual sections or chapters: Robert Ford, Jennifer Riddle Harding, Emma Kafalenos, R. B. Kershner, and Gerald Prince. As always, Sangeeta Ray helped me greatly at several levels, scholarly, professional, and personal. Finally, particular thanks go to Jim Phelan and Peter Rabinowitz, who deserve a special narratological term such as Superreader for their hard work, generous advice, and brilliant editing.

Earlier versions of Chapters Two, Four, and Six appeared in *Genre* 24 (1991) 309–30; *Style* 28 (1994) 312–28; and *New Literary History* 28 (2001) 681–94. I thank these journals for permission to reproduce this material.

Introduction

TRANSGRESSING SELF AND VOICE—CONTEMPORARY FICTION AND THE DEATH OF THE NARRATOR

chapter one

In 1954, Wolfgang Kayser warned that if we lose sight of the fact that the narrator is "someone" who "tells a story," the novel is dead: "The death of the narrator is the death of the novel" (34).[1] As it would turn out, Kayser could not have been more wrong. Narrative literature was about to explode with a wide range of post-anthropomorphic narrators while philosophy (soon to be followed by critical theory) was beginning its half-century assault on humanism. The significance of this shift should not be minimized—by moving beyond merely human narrators, texts begin to tamper with or destroy outright the "mimetic contract" that had governed conventional fiction for centuries: no more can one assume that a first person narrator would resemble a normal human being, with all its abilities and limitations (excepting, of course, a never-remarked-upon ability to produce a highly narratable story that reads just like a novel).

If we look back on the broadest trajectories of the history of the use of the narrator in fiction it will become apparent that such a move was probably inevitable. Two main features stand out in the development of fictional technique since Defoe: the exploration of subjectivity (beginning with Sterne's play with unexpected associations of ideas and continuing with Jane Austen's development of free indirect discourse); the other is the rise of the unreliable narrator, which had been present in epistolary fiction and gained new prominence by the time Dostoevsky's "Notes from the Underground" (1864) appeared.

In addition, narrative fragmentation and unexpected reconstructions, begun by Sterne in *Tristram Shandy* (1767), were redeployed by a number of Romantic authors including Byron (*Don Juan,* 1824), Heine (*Buch le Grand,* 1827), Pushkin (*Evgeny Onegin,* 1833), and in numerous works of Jean Paul.

Each of these developments suggests further steps along the same path: one goes from unreliable narrators to incompetent ones to delusional and then completely insane storytellers. One starts with flawed narration, goes on to more fragmented forms, and ends with the semi-coherent and utterly opaque. The represented consciousness is increasingly abnormal: we move from Woolf's Septimus Smith to Faulkner's Benjy to Beckett's Molloy to Nabokov's Charles Kinbote. The first person narrator with a full name and clear identity in earlier fiction becomes one who implies pseudonymity by stating, "Call me Ishmael"; the next move is the anonymous narrator of the "Cyclops" episode of *Ulysses* (1922) followed by the unnamed though intimate narrator of *Invisible Man* (1953) who, it might be noted, mentions that The Brotherhood had him change his name but never informs us of either the old or the new name. In Beckett's *The Unnamable* (1953), there is simply a disembodied voice that does not have a name; this movement culminates in the multiple dubious narrators collapsed together in the more extreme *nouveaux romans.*

With virtually all earlier fiction having been written in either the first or third person, how could experimental writers fail to move on to the "we" form that combines them, or the "you" that confuses them, and then go on to explore the possibilities of narration from the perspective of "they," "one," a pronounless passive voice, and new, invented pronouns until one reaches the anthology of pronominal forms that make up Maurice Roche's *Compact* (1966)? In what follows, I will begin by indicating the large range of the unusual narrators and consciousnesses of contemporary fiction, go on to address particular questions of narrative theory posed by these odd words, and discuss unusual pronominal forms and comment on their functions, thereby preparing the way for the extended accounts of second, first person plural, and multiperson narration that will take up the three chapters that follow. Finally I will attempt to categorize some prominent types of non- and anti-mimetic narration.

The kinds of posthuman narrators that have appeared in the last several decades are protean. In addition to the demented narrators of Beckett or the mute storytellers in Calvino's *The Castle of Crossed Destinies* (1969), we find, to note only some of the most prominent cases, voluble corpses (Beckett's "The Calmative," 1946), impossibly eloquent children (in John Hawkes' *Virginie: Her Two Lives,* 1981), a ghost whose narrative is unreliable in Kurosawa's *Rashomon* (1951), sophisticated storytelling animals (a horse in John Hawkes' *Sweet William,* 1993), the Cretan Minotaur in Borges's "The House of Asturion" (1949), a disembodied voice that narrates compulsively (Beckett's *The Unnamable*), a mind that can perceive the unspoken thoughts of many others (Rushdie's Saleem Sinai, 1981), a television set that appears to display the confused memories of the protagonist (Grass' *Local Anaesthetic,* 1969), a cybernetic device that allows one person to experience virtually the perceptions of another (Gibson's *Neuromancer,* 1984), and even storytelling machines (in Stanisław Lem's *The Cyberiad,* 1967). In a trajectory that will frequently appear in the pages that follow, we will note how reflection on a typically postmodern practice can stimulate literary historical reflections that yield unexpected antecedents: narration from the other side of the grave is found at least as far back as Machado de Assis' *The Posthumous Memoirs of Brás Cubas* (1881), while bestial narrators and focalizers (whose function is not merely allegorical) stretch back to Tolstoy's story "Kholstomer" (1886) as well as Virginia Woolf's literal snail's-eye-view of the events in "Kew Gardens" (1919).[2] It should be readily apparent that a model centered on storytelling situations in real life cannot begin to do justice to these narrators who become ever more extravagantly anti-realistic every decade.

Play with the real or imagined gender of the narrator has also been a staple of contemporary fiction, especially gender impersonation, transformation, and obfuscation, and this has produced its share of critical puzzlement. "Stream of consciousness" writing, or "autonomous interior monologue," as Dorrit Cohn more precisely terms it, has been unable to resist impersonating the mind of the other gender since the origin of this practice. I am referring not only to Molly Bloom's monologue but to Schnitzler's early psychonarration, the 1924 novella,

"Fräulein Else." Since these texts appeared, numerous authors have attempted such sustained transgendered representations, including Coetzee's *Foe* (1986), which simultaneously provides a woman's narration (which is doomed to be suppressed) and resolutely refuses to narrate or otherwise speak for the African character, Friday. Likewise, the assiduous, realistic, and decidedly male first person narrator of Julian Barnes' 1984 novel, *Flaubert's Parrot,* abruptly gives way in the eleventh chapter to the obviously fictive first person narration of Flaubert's lover, Louise Colet, who offers to provide the other half of the story. Other, more radical play with gender includes the strange first person narration of Evelyn, the man who will be made (against his will) into a biological woman in Angela Carter's *The Passion of New Eve* (1977), and whose consciousness and narration will be transformed as completely as his/her body is.

The strategy that causes the most consternation among conventional readers, however, is the refusal to identify the gender of the narrator, especially when the narrator is involved in sexual acts. This situation is provocatively foregrounded in Jeanette Winterson's *Written on the Body* (1992). As Susan S. Lanser observes in her discussion of sex, gender, and narration, "the unnamed autodiegetic narrator of [this book] is never identified as male or female"; since the plot revolves around the narrator's love of a married woman (and, before that relationship has begun, the narrator has sexual relationships with both male and female characters), "that silence and the extent to which it destabilizes both textuality and sexuality drive this novel at least as much as its surface plot" ("Queering" 250). This situation also appears in June Arnold's *The cook and the carpenter: a novel by the carpenter* (1973), where the characters are referred to exclusively by an invented, genderless pronoun, "na." Since the cook and the carpenter form a union, a similar dynamic of reception develops until the gender of the characters is revealed at the end of the text. Needless to say, these works appear to refute the speculation of a few narratologists like Mieke Bal (122) who argue that since narrators are verbal constructs rather than actual people, they are not gendered and therefore should properly be termed "it" rather than "he" or "she." After all, being a fictional construct does not mean being ungendered: many fictional entities from unicorns to divine beings to implied authors are quite definitively gendered.[3]

Another seminal transformation that has occurred involves the relations between author and narrator. Since early modernist fiction (if not before), it has been crucial to differentiate carefully between the author and the narrator of a work, and never to assume uncritically that the speaker of the text represents the ideas of its author. The concept of the unreliable narrator, a foundational modernist type of narrator, presupposes such a clear division. "Marcel" in *In Search of Lost Time* is not Marcel Proust, and Stephen Dedalus, when he writes in the first person at the end of *Portrait of the Artist as a Young Man,* is not identical with James Joyce. This distinction, which furthermore helped give rise to the concept of the implied author, is often eroded or assaulted by many postmodern authors, who cannot resist interpolating characters who bear their own names and life history into the fictional world they have created. In many cases, these incursions are largely innocuous ontologically; they differ little from Chaucer's depiction of a bad storyteller named Chaucer in "The Tale of Sir Tophas." They are, that is, fictional characters that resemble their authors just as a character called Napoleon or Richard Nixon in a fictional text may (or may not) resemble the historical original but is in the final analysis merely a fictional construct. Other such incarnations, however, are much more transgressive of this boundary. Some of Nabokov's stories, such as "First Love," were published both as fiction and as autobiography. The work of W. G. Sebald glides in and out of the categories of documentary prose, essayistic reflection, and narrative fiction. The author of the nonfictional preface of Nabokov's *Bend Sinister* asserts he is the governing intelligence of the text that is dimly perceived by his protagonist. Kurt Vonnegut incorporates his personal testimony of the Allied firebombing of Dresden into an antiwar novel, and affirms the historical accuracy of his descriptions and the identity of the character Vonnegut and the author: "That was me. That was the author of this book" (125).[4]

Still more relevant to this study are the many odd, unusual, or impossible speakers found in contemporary works. These figures are also much more challenging to traditional narrative theory, which is typically based on the mimesis of actual speech situations. If a narrative is, as commonly averred, someone relating a set of events to someone else, then this entire way of looking at narrative has to be reconsidered in the light of the numerous ways innovative authors problematize each term of this formula, especially the first one. Summing up nearly all of the theorizing on "point of view" since the time of Henry James and Victor Shklovsky, Gérard Genette writes that the novelist must choose between two narrative postures, either "to have the story told by one of its 'characters,' or to have it told by a narrator outside the story" (*Narrative* 244). It is, however, precisely this choice that is rejected by so many contemporary authors. As we will see in some detail in the next chapter, second person prose is perhaps exemplary in this respect; the "you" invoked will at different points seem to be one of the characters; at others a narrator outside the story; it may furthermore seem to refer to a narratee or the actual reader who holds the book. We find this blurring of person cunningly represented in one of the "you" passages in Fuentes' *La Muerta de Artemio Cruz:* "Cuando Catalina pegue el oído a la puerta que los separa y esuche tus movimentos; cuando tú, del otro lado de la puerta, te muevas sin saber que eras escuchado, sin saber alguíen vive pendiente de los ruidos y los silencios de tu vida detrás de la puerta, ¿quién vivirá en esa separacíon?" (1115). ("When Catalina puts her ear to the door that separates her from you and listens to your movements; when you, on the other side of the door, move without knowing that someone hangs upon the sounds and silences of your life: who will live in that separation?" [30]). It is precisely the space between the perceiver and the perceived over which the "you" narration hovers. Revealingly, Genette goes on to express his consternation at the new fiction that "does not hesitate to establish between narrator and character(s) a variable or floating relationship, a pronominal vertigo in tune with a freer logic and a more complex 'personality'" (246). It is precisely this "logic" that needs to be investigated, and this "vertigo" that needs to be savored.

We might then begin by emphasizing that much recent fiction rejects a mimetic model. Thus, a conventional work like *Roxana* or *Great Expectations* is modeled on the nonfictional genre of the memoir or autobiography. Its narrator can only know what an autobiographer can know, and must remain ignorant of other minds as well as of facts that s/he has not learned (such as the contents of private meetings by discreet individuals). This is why, for example, Dorrit Cohn, following Philippe Lejeune, states that first person works of fiction can be differentiated from autobiographies only by explicit, usually paratextual indications of fictionality or if the name of the narrator differs from that of the author (*Distinction* 58–60).[5]

Likewise, a traditional, mimetic third person fiction will typically follow the basic conventions of biography or the history of a family, with the exception that the narrator is able to know what goes on in the minds of one or more characters.[6] A first person narrator cannot know what is in the minds of others, and a third person narrator may perform this, and a few other such acts, but may not stray beyond the established conventions of depicting such perceptions: the thought of one character may not be lodged within the mind of another without any intervening plausible explanation. These rules, however, have always been more frail and arbitrary than narrative theorists have usually wanted to acknowledge. Nikolai Gogol in his 1842 story, "The Overcoat," draws attention to both of these conventions. As his protagonist is strolling in the streets of St. Petersburg at night in his new overcoat, he sees a salacious figurine in a shop window and smiles. The narrator asks a few rhetorical questions concerning the cause of this smile, before going on to aver that there is no creeping into a man's soul and finding out what he thinks. Throughout the text, however, he has been doing just that, revealing private thoughts, disclosing scenes that were unobserved, and generally assuming the prerogatives of a third person narrator—even as he complains that his memory is growing dim and he cannot recall all the details of the events he narrates. Gogol is obviously mocking these conventions and refusing to be bound by them; he is clearly telling his reader that when it comes to narration, he can do whatever he pleases—a sentiment many current novelists obviously share. Even the high modernists who perfected the verisimilar presentation of an individual consciousness could not resist violating these basic rules. Proust's Marcel knows what transpires in Swann's mind as well as any third person narrator could, and Joyce could not resist planting a few stray private thoughts of one individual within the consciousness of an unwitting other in the later parts of *Ulysses* (see Peake 268–69).

We can get a sense of some of these developments in the practice of narration and the representation of consciousness by glancing briefly at the way Alain Robbe-Grillet treats these related issues at different points in his career. His first stories seem to be unconnected, hyper-objective acts of pure description; each in fact plays with different facets of perception. "In the Corridors of the Metro" (1959) is typical in this regard and represents a distillation of the techniques of many of the early short texts, beginning with "Three Reflected Visions" (1954): "Corridors" can be read as a series of inconsequential descriptions and unrelated events or, if a single perceiving subject is postulated, we have continuous narrative progression as seen through the eyes of a mobile though unmentioned focalizer. "The Way Back" (1954) is a brief story that is significant for its exploration of the possibilities of "we" narration. In *Le Voyeur,* Robbe-Grillet's second published novel (1955), the rather ordinary thoughts of a certain Mathias are set forth minute by minute for a third of the book. A blank page in the text then appears. Afterwards, we learn that a terrible crime has been committed, and

Matthias seeks desperately to fill the void represented by those missing minutes. It is up to the reader to fill in the literally unspeakable crime that Mathias has clearly committed, thereby becoming the "voyeur" of the title.

In his next novel, *La Jalousie* (1957), Robbe-Grillet employs what has been termed the *je-néant* or absent-I narrator. As Dorrit Cohn points out, "the changing angles of vision and spatial distances, the obsessive repetitions of language and scene, insistently prompt the reader to postulate a human eye (and 'I') behind the voice—not just a camera eye" (*Transparent* 207) All the events of this text are indeed perceived through the eyes of a figure who is never named or referred to, and whose existence must be deduced from obscure hints hidden within the descriptions, including those noted by Cohn. We have, as it were, individualized perception without an identified perceiver. The inferred perceiver, the jealous husband, is certainly the sole focalizer of the text, and may or may not be its narrator, since it is not certain that he is responsible for the words of the book. Here we have instead, as in "In The Corridors of the Metro," a most unusual figure that we might name the "hidden focalizer"; Robbe-Grillet's works from this period simultaneously flirt with an arch objectivism that goes far beyond the "camera eye" technique of a Dos Passos or Isherwood and also present an unusual, extreme subjectivity with a minimum of mediation. The work can be viewed, that is, as the epitome of either narrational objectivity or subjectivity.

In *Dans le labyrinthe* (1959), Robbe-Grillet ties up a confusing series of self-negating narrative strands by abruptly announcing that a minor character in the story, the doctor, is in fact its narrator; this is very possibly a parody of a similar stratagem that had just been enacted by Camus (which I will shortly discuss). The narrator of *La Maison de rendez-vous* (1965) is, like every other figure in the text, something of a cardboard figure that imperfectly represents a human being. His narration is filled with contradictions, repetitions, and variations that, as a character in the world he depicts, he cannot begin to explain. Finally, in the flagrantly and self-consciously contradictory narrative that makes up *Projet pour une révolution à New York* (1970), two men are seen in the bushes bordering a park. One character asks a thirteen-year-old who they are; the girl responds: "That's easy: one is Ben-Said, the other is the narrator" (57). We have come to the end of a trajectory; the narrator now is only an empty name to be parodied.

§

The third person is not what it used to be. Roland Barthes' denunciation of it, despite his playfully extreme language, is fairly representative of its fall from favor among modernist and postmodern writers as well as theorists writing after Lubbock and Sartre. Barthes (*Barthes*) states: "'he' is nasty: it is the nastiest word in the language: the pronoun of the non-person, it nullifies and mortifies its referent; . . . If I say 'he' of someone, I always have in mind a sort of murder by language" (171). Other theorists like Audrey Jaffe, William Nelles ("Omnisicence"), and Jonathan Culler have recently qualified or debated the traditional notion of omniscience; as Culler states, "the fundamental point is that since we do not know whether there is a God and what she might know, divine omniscience is not a model that helps us think about authors or about literary narration" (23). In another sphere, Dorrit Cohn (*Distinction* 132–49) and Margot Norris (216–36) show how the third person narrators of Thomas Mann and James Joyce display a demonstrable and idiosyncratic subjectivity that often makes them less than fully reliable. Indeed, Joyce's third person narrations regularly incarnate what Hugh Kenner has called "the Uncle Charles principle," in which the discourse of the narrator is infiltrated by language typical of the character being described, as we may observe in the opening sentence of "The Dead": "Lily, the caretaker's daughter, was literally run off her feet"; the words she might use to describe herself here find their way into the pen of the narrator.[7] Gordon Collier likewise examines "subjectivized third person narration" in Patrick White's *The Solid Mandala,* introducing a critical term that we should probably expect to see more widely used in studies to come.

These examples do not begin to exhaust the many possibilities that recent writers have brought into being. Hypertext narrators further problematize the idea of omniscience and even of third person narration by creating a series of narrative possibilities that a reader must then convert into a single story, one which, by definition, cannot have been fully known in advance of its reading. And, as we will see in a later chapter, Beckett and others demonstrate how third person narrators can erase the narrative world they have just created. In his essay, "To Write: An Intransitive Verb?," Roland Barthes resurrected the archaic linguistic form of "the middle voice," which indicates the speaking subject is affected by the action depicted by the verb, to represent the practice of the modern *scripteur,* and Brian Macaskill (1994) and Mario Ortiz-Robles (2004) have shown how this concept can be employed in the analysis of specific narratives. Another recent theoretical essay should be mentioned here, Henrik Nielsen's analysis of the impersonal voice in first person fiction, which argues compellingly that in literary fiction, "one cannot be certain that it is the person referred to as 'I' who speaks or narrates, and therefore . . . we need to posit an impersonal voice of the narrative" (133). If some theorists are demonstrating the subjectivity of much third person fiction, others are complicating our notion of first person narration.

And what of the opposition itself? The distinction Genette finds so foundational (and which Stanzel and others cover by referring to fundamental first and third person narrative standpoints) is one which many recent writers cannot resist inverting. Since these playful joustings with this convention deserve to be better known, I will take a couple of pages to delineate some of the more interesting transgressions. At the end of Camus' *La Peste* (1947), as Didier Husson (1991) has noted, the narrator who has guided us through the novel reveals himself to be the principal character, Dr. Rieux; for the entirety of the novel he has disguised his identity and spoken of himself in the third person. Robbe-Grillet's more radical appropriation of this move in *Dans le labyrinthe,* which changes the novel from a heterodiegetic to a homodiegetic one, calls into question the real significance of a relation that can be altered so easily. In other works that utilize this device for different purposes, we might even state that part of the plot is the determination of the true identity of the narrator's relation to the discourse. In "The Shape of the Sword" (1944), Borges' protagonist recounts, in the third person, the story of a cowardly traitor; only by the end of the tale do we realize that the narrator has been describing himself all along. Genette, we may note in passing, discusses this example in *Narrative Discourse* (243–47) only to conclude, rather strangely, that "the Borgesian fantastic, in this respect emblematic of a whole modern literature, does not accept person" (247). This statement is clearly false; the plot of the story and its reception is precisely about the consequences of person in narration. We may term this specific practice a "pseudo–third person" narrative, and identify a dramatic analogue in Beckett's appropriately titled short play, "Not I," in which a monologist appears to be speaking about another but is in fact unwittingly referring to scenes from her own life. The same strategy also appears in other works of these two authors, as we will see; for now we may simply point to Beckett's *Company,* a text that constitutes a sustained, self-conscious exploration of pronominal positions, as the alternation between a "you" and a "he" is revealed in the end to be a spurious distinction, a futile attempt by an isolated individual to engender company.[8]

Another text that contains abrupt revelations or complications of the actual gendered identity of the narrator is Calvino's *The Nonexistent Knight* (1959). At the beginning, it is a third-person narrative of the postmodern adventures of several of Charlemagne's paladins, including Raimbaut's pursuit of the amazonian warrior, Bradamante. Some thirty pages into the novella, however, the author of the narrative makes her presence known and reveals herself to be a nun in a convent who is trying to imagine the foreign scenes she recounts. At the end of the text she again employs the first person and discloses that she is in fact the very Bradamante she had been describing in the third person—and as the object of a male quest. The strategy of narration thus tends to negate the ideological valence implicit in the story's teleology, that of the (con)quest of the female. Once again, a third person text is abruptly transformed into a more subjective narrative perspective. This innovation in narration is much more widespread in practice than is generally acknowledged. Novels by Anthony Powell (*A Dance to the Music of Time,* 1975), Doris Lessing's 1962 novel, *The Golden Notebook* (as interpreted by Beth Boehm), Margaret Drabble (*The Waterall,* 1969), Margaret Atwood (*The Blind Assassin,* 2000), and, most flagrantly, Ian McEwan (*Atonement,* 2001) also include this transformation.[9] And as Suzanne Keen explains, in Iris Murdoch's *The Philosopher's Pupil* (1983), the narrator first appears to be a traditional third person teller, but is revealed in the end to be "involved in the action with the characters of the story world. Evidently, 'N' has interviewed all the participants in order to gain the copious evidence of their thoughts, feelings, and motivations that would usually be plausible only as funneled through an external authorial narrator" (41). Murdoch, that is, demonstrates how a first person narrator might possibly, within the bounds of realism, write accurately as a third person teller seemingly privy to the thoughts of others. The other narrators tend to be rather less scrupulous concerning the sources of their apparent knowledge of other minds; in the case of McEwan this produces a kind of pseudo-focalization in which the thoughts of several individuals are presented as if by an omniscient third person narrator, but it is one who turns out to be merely a character who uses her imagination to attempt to intuit the probable or possible thoughts of the others.[10]

The same move can be made with the second person. In Joyce Carol Oates's story "You" (1970), we are presented with what I would call a pseudo-second person narrative. The first third of the story seems to be a straightforward example of what I will call standard second person narration, in which the protagonist, focalizer, and governing consciousness of the text is a single figure designated by the second person pronoun. Such an assumption is strengthened by narration that seems to depict the stream of thoughts of the titular character: "It strikes you that this is an important scene, an emotional scene. People are watching you anxiously. You might be in a play. Not one of those crappy television plays . . ." (365). A little more than a third of the way into the story, however, a first person narrator emerges; it turns out that the tale's narrator is the neglected teenage daughter, and the "you" refers entirely to the daughter's imaginative construction of the probable events, physical and mental, of her mother's life. Once again, the plot of the narrative and the poignancy of the events turn on the revelation of the narrator's actual identity, as the text's play with the conventions of narration and its reception is disclosed.

All of these examples follow the same logic: the nature and identity of the narrator becomes itself a miniature drama as a familiar narrating situation is established throughout the text only to be utterly transformed at the end. The heterodiegetic narrator outside the story turns out to have been in there all along; the seemingly daring narrative "you" is instead a more conventional apostrophe, the story of another is revealed to be the story of oneself. The conventional practice is deployed until it is turned inside out, revealing the artificiality of a perspective, whether designated "third person" or "heterodiegetic," that can be so easily inverted. And it will be noted that the move is always away from traditional objectivity and omniscience, from the third person to the first.[11] The foundation that Genette and others would use to ground their models of narrative is far more tenuous than usually imagined, and only lasts until the whim of the author intervenes. As Michel Butor has clarified in one of his theoretical essays, "in the novel [the] distinction between the three grammatical persons is much less rigorous than it can be in everyday life; they are linked to each other" (*Inventory* 62).[12] Or, to draw on a self-reflexive statement on this subject by one of Beckett's speakers in *Stories and Texts for Nothing* that articulates the fluidity (and, perhaps, the possible arbitrariness) of such differentiations: "it wonders, that voice which is silence, or it's me, there's no telling, it's all the same dream, the same silence, it and me, it and him, him and me, and all our train, and all theirs, and all theirs" (139).

In contemporary fiction, one narration is collapsed into another, and one consciousness bleeds into a second one, or a foreign text inscribes itself on a mind. These anti-mimetic interpenetrations can take numerous forms, such as the extremely odd third person narration of much of Beckett's *Watt* (1953) which is abruptly "claimed" by a first person narrator, Sam, halfway through the book—an act which unmoors both narrative perspectives since a character narrator should not have been able to produce the text we have been reading up to the point of his admission of authorship. An extreme, metaleptic form of this conflation appears in Borges' story "The Circular Ruins" (1940), which culminates in the protagonist's realization that he and his thoughts are an illusion, that someone else is dreaming him. Still other types of contaminated subjectivities will be noted in the description of "conflated narrators" below.

Narrators can diverge from normal human speakers in still more ways. The narrator at the beginning of Caryl Phillips' *Crossing the River*, a novel composed of four novellas separated in time and space, opens with a preface narrated by one who states: "For two hundred years I have listened to the many-tongued chorus. And occasionally, among the sundry restless voices, I have discovered those of my own children" (1). The narrative further contains interpolations of one speaker's thoughts within the mind of another, temporally distant speaker, planted there not by any naturalistic knowledge or preternatural telepathy, but simply by a daring auctorial fiat. This gesture both conveys the sense of a traditional tribute to the ancestors and explores the realm of a posthuman sensibility which, according to Katheryn Hayles, "privileges informational pattern over material instantiation" (2); it can serve as a foretaste of the kinds of extreme acts of narration I will cover in this book.

Up to this point, I have tried to identify the most interesting and striking deployments of voice, perspective, and narration over the past fifty years. These are not random changes; we can in fact observe a number of distinct yet complementary trajectories these innovations have taken. There is a general move away from what was thought to be "omniscient" third person narration to limited third person narration to ever more unreliable first person narrators to new explorations of "you," "we," and mixed forms. There is a similar movement from the psychological novel to more impressionistic renderings of consciousness to the dissolution of consciousness into textuality, and a corresponding move from human-like narrators to quasi-human, non-human, and anti-human speakers, as the figure of the narrator as a recognizable human being recedes into an ever greater eclipse. The basic categories of first and third person narration or homo- and heterodiegesis, themselves based on foundational linguistic oppositions articulated by Benveniste, are repeatedly problematized and violated by experimental writers. For the most part neither of the major theoretical approaches can begin to comprehend this plethora of new work for the simple reason that it rejects the type of mimetic representation that both theories presuppose.

The rest of this book is intended to provide broad analyses, working models, and theoretical conceptualizations of this neglected twentieth-century tradition of non- and anti-mimetic fiction. In the remaining paragraphs of this chapter, I will describe the range of pronominal perspectives that have been employed in narration in recent years, and then go on to devote a chapter each to the three most important forms: second person, first person plural, and multiperson modes.[13] This analysis will conclude with a flexible model of the varieties of contemporary narration at the end of the fourth chapter. The second part of the book will go on to explore a number of other salient and even more transgressive techniques typical of postmodernism before setting forth a workable model of the narrative transaction capacious enough to include these unruly practices.

We may begin with the two most widespread, important, and perhaps unnerving narrational stances: the "you" and the "we" forms. Among the virtues of these pronominal stances is the protean range of each: "you" is particularly devious, since it can refer to the protagonist, the narrator, the narratee, or the reader; authors using this form regularly play on this ambiguity as well as on its multiple possible meanings. It also can be used in three different ways: in its standard form, it designates a protagonist, oscillating between the functions of the first and the third person. It can also approximate the ordinary function of the pronoun "one" in its "recipe" function (e.g., "Begin by meeting him in a class, a bar, a rummage sale"); finally, this pronominal form can also refer to the reader holding the book. "We" is fluid in a different way; it can grow or shrink to accommodate very different sized groups and can either include or exclude the reader. It too, though in a more subtle manner, also typically rejects the basic dyad of first and third person.

Other forms are considerably less common but equally interesting. In *L'Opoponax* (1964), Monique Wittig has written a novel from the perspective of "one" *(on)*; ironically, it was translated into English as a "you" narration (to the horror of the author), as if it was felt that the "one" narration would be too alienating. The German equivalent, *man*, is dominant in many successive paragraphs near the beginning of Adalbert Stifter's "Bergkristall" (1845); Fludernik notes that there are three novels that extensively employ this mode, the first of which is Joseph Roth's *Radetzkymarsch* (1932).[14] Third person forms have also seen some interesting variations. Joseph Conrad and Maurice Roche, as we will see below, have sections of their works written in a passive voice that dissolves the agency of individual characters. There are brief "it" passages, as Fludernik has noted, in Christopher Isherwood's *A Single Man* and in John Fowles' *Mantissa;* these also appear in the work of Beckett. Other works depict a collective subject largely or entirely designated by the pronoun "they": D. H. Lawrence's story "Things," George Perec's similarly named novel *Les Choses,* two chapters of Mary McCarthy's *The Group,* and Monique Wittig's novel *Les Guérillères*, and much of the discourse of Nathalie Sarraute's later novels refers almost exclusively to a "they." Wittig's subject is further limited to the female "they" form (*elles*) that is possible in French. Other feminist authors have further extended the parameters of third person fiction. June Arnold, in *The cook and the carpenter,* created a gender neutral pronoun, "Na," to refer to all people regardless of gender. Kathy Acker's story "Humiliation" (1990) is written entirely in a prose devoid of pronouns that thwarts individual agency ("Since wanted to be a writer, tried to find her own voice. Couldn't. But still loved to write. Loved to play with language" [115]) and is thus perfectly suited to embody the story's titular theme and oscillates oddly between first and third person perspectives. Finally, we should also observe how a traditional narrative stance, "I," can be transformed and defamiliarized by dividing the letters that compose the word in French (*j/e*), as Monique Wittig does in *Le Corps lesbien* (1973) as she once again seeks a form of narration that will represent a distinct female experience.

In almost all books that center on narration, there comes a point when the theorist notes that what is meant by first or third person narration is not the pronoun being used, but the position of the narrator. Thus, autobiographies written in the third person such as Caesar's *Gallic Wars* or *The Education of Henry Adams* are nevertheless related from a first person standpoint; likewise, one may address oneself in the second person without transcending the normal boundaries of the position of the first person. This is equally the case with still stranger examples such as Henry James' awkward use of "one" to refer to himself at the beginning of *The American Scene* or Rimbaud's use of "he" to designate a past self the writer felt he had discarded. I cannot, however, make the same confident claim with all the examples I am assembling here. I am not certain what to do with Kathy Acker's essentially pronounless narration, that intimate presentation of a single subjectivity that occasionally uses a third person genitive pronoun, such as "her." One presumes that this kind of narration would normally occupy a third person position, though in this example Acker seems to be making it do the normal work of the first person. This ambiguity is precisely the point of the story: her practice thus represents an evacuation of agency. We will pause here and treat this and the more extreme examples just noted as typical instances of the conceptual indeterminability and defamiliarizing power of such innovative techniques that will be discussed at length in the three chapters that follow.

"At First You Feel a Bit Lost"

THE VARIETIES OF SECOND PERSON NARRATION

chapter two

The genealogy of second person fiction is surprisingly rich, including Nathaniel Hawthorne's story "The Haunted Mind" (1835), Hans Christian Andersen's brief sketch "This Fable Is Intended for You" (1836), the opening sections of May Sinclair's *Mary Olivier* (1919), the sixth chapter of Part Two of Jean Rhys's *After Leaving Mr. Mackenzie* (1931), Mary McCarthy's "The Genial Host" (1941), Ilse Aichinger's "Spiegelgeschichte" (1954), as well as, intriguingly enough, Rex Stout's detective novel *How Like a God* (1929) and the first sentence of the nineteenth chapter of Ian Fleming's first James Bond novel, *Casino Royale* (1953): "You are about to awaken when you dream that you are dreaming" (124).[1] Since the publication of Michel Butor's *La Modification* in 1957, second person narrative became much more visible on the literary landscape, especially those areas occupied by experimental authors. The nineteen sixties and the early seventies saw the publication of a number of interesting texts written in the second person, including Carlos Fuentes' *Aura* (1962), the first chapter of John Hawkes' *The Lime Twig* (1962), Georges Perec's *Un Homme qui dort* (1967), Mark Insingel's *Reflections* (1968), John McGahern's *The Dark* (1969), Edna O'Brien's *A Pagan Place* (1970), W. S. Merwin's "The Second Person" (1970), and several passages of Thomas Pynchon's *Gravity's*

Rainbow (1973). It was not, however, until the early nineties that second person narration received extended theoretical study.

In what follows, I will attempt to identify the main types of second person narrative, differentiate them from superficially similar forms, discuss their status, and show how they achieve their distinctive effects. I will distinguish three types of second person narrative: what I will call 1) the "standard," 2) the "hypothetical," and 3) the "autotelic" forms. The standard form is by far the most common, and will consequently receive the most attention in what follows. It can be identified by its designation of the protagonist as "you," rather than "I," "he" or "she"; its best known example is Michel Butor's *La Modification* (1957). The hypothetical form employs the style of the guidebook to recount a narrative, as in several of Lorrie Moore's stories: "Begin by meeting him in a class" ("How" 55). The autotelic form employs direct address to the reader or narratee, as in the opening of Italo Calvino's *If on a winter's night a traveller:* "You are about to begin reading Italo Calvino's new novel." In the course of this analysis, I will try to clarify the shifting relationships that the second person has with its more established and conventional neighbors, the first and third persons, and speculate on the social, literary, and philosophical reasons behind the emergence and proliferation of this technique in our time. Finally, I will discuss analogues of this practice in other genres.

First, however, it is necessary to distinguish second person narrative from other types of fiction that frequently employ the second person pronoun at the level of narration. One of these is the familiar authorial colloquy in which a heterodiegetic narratee ("gentle reader") is directly addressed, a common practice of Fielding, Thackeray, and George Eliot. Another kind of narrative that frequently employs the word "you" but that is not properly speaking a second person narrative is the monologue addressed to a real or imaginary homodiegetic audience, works like Camus' *La Chute* and Hawkes' *Travesty.* An additional conventional type of text that uses the second person pronoun with considerable frequency is the apostrophe; such texts likewise present little problem for narrative theory and are readily situated within standard categories of narrative and rhetorical analysis.[2] All these works can be easily comprehended by traditional dyadic theories of narration point of view: the authorial colloquy exists outside of the narrative proper, the autobiographical monologue and apostrophe are addressed to characters, albeit silent or absent ones, within the fictional world.

Even after delimiting the field in this way, we find a wide variety of second person texts. We may define second person narrative as any narration other than an apostrophe that designates its protagonist by a second person pronoun. This protagonist will usually be the sole focalizer, and is often (but not always) the work's principal narratee as well. This definition accords with that of Monika Fludernik ("Introduction" 288); it differs from those proffered by Gerald Prince (86) and Matt DelConte in which the "you" simultaneously designates both the protagonist and the narratee. In some cases, such as in several passages of O'Brien's *A Pagan Place,* the narratee is quite distinct from the "you" protagonist: "Alone for the first time on the street, you were conscious of your appearance. Your coat was ridiculous compared to other people's coats" (172). The use of "you," the past tense, and the suggestion that the character is being seen externally show that this is decidedly not the kind of speech a character would normally direct to herself. As David Herman remarks on this passage, "textual *you* functions not (or not only) as discourse particle relaying and linking the various components of a fictional protagonist's self-address, but (also) as a form of address that exceeds the frame of the fiction itself" (342). A still more obvious discrepancy (indeed, an unbridgeable one) between narrator, protagonist, and narratee appears in Calvino's 1984 story, "A King Listens": "Around you there is no longer a palace, there is the night filled with cries and shouts. Where are you? Are you still alive? Have you eluded the assassins who have burst into the throne room? Did the secret stairway afford you an avenue of escape?" (59). These rhetorical questions are not literally addressed to the protagonist, but rather directed to an extradiegetic narratee.

It is important to note that second person narration is an artificial mode that does not normally occur in natural narrative or in most texts in the history of literature before 1919. In most instances, the story is narrated in the present tense, and one type, the "hypothetical" or "recipe" form, also includes frequent usage of conditional and future tenses. It should also be noted that my account enumerates tendencies rather than stipulates invariant conditions; this is because second person narration is an extremely protean form, and its very essence is to eschew a fixed essence.

I. The Standard Form

The most common type of second person narrative, what I term the "standard" form, is also the closest to more traditional forms of narration. In it, a story is told, usually in the present tense, about a single protagonist who is referred to in the second person; the "you" often designates the narrator and the narratee as well, though as we will see there is considerable slippage in this unusual triumvirate. This is the form used in *La Modification, Aura, Un Homme qui dort, A Pagan Place,* and Jay McInerney's *Bright Lights, Big City.* Butor is often mistakenly credited with having invented the technique; as we have seen there are several earlier short stories which are written entirely in the second person. A typical passage from McCarthy's "The Genial Host" reads: "Now you hesitated, weighing the invitation. Sooner or later you would break with him, you knew. But not yet, not while you were still so poor, so loverless, so lonely" (163). The opening lines of Aichinger's text also provide an excellent example of this form: "Wenn einer dein Bett aus dem Saal schiebt, wenn du siehst, dass der Himmel grün wird, und wenn du dem Vikar die Leichenrede ersparen willst, so ist es Zeit fur dich, aufzustehen, leise. . . ." (44). ("When someone pushes your bed out of the ward, when you see that the sky is growing green and when you want to save the priest the trouble of holding a funeral service, then it is time for you to get up, softly. . . ." [Aldridge, 65–66]).

These sentences could have been written in the first person, in the third person with a single focalizer, or in free indirect speech. Instead, the second person was chosen, and a different type of narration follows, one which approximates but cannot be reduced to any of these other perspectives. Some of its characteristic features include ambiguity over the identity and status of the "you": it is, at the outset, epistemologically a more dubious pronoun than the traditional "I" or "she," which we ordinarily have no trouble processing as we encounter a fictional text for the first time. The "you" (or in the case of Aichinger, "du") also threatens the ontological stability of the fictional world insofar as it seems it could be addressing the reader as well as the central character. In standard second person fiction (unlike other second person forms), the protagonist/narratee is quite distinct from the actual or implied reader; nevertheless, one of the more unsettling features of this mode of narration is that this distinction can be collapsed whenever the "you" could refer to the reader as well as the protagonist.

Most authors employing this mode play with this boundary. In *Un Homme qui dort,* Perec writes: "Tu as vingt-cinq ans et vingt-neuf dents, trois chemises et huit chausettes, quelques livres que tu ne lis plus, quelque disques que tu n'ecoutes plus" ("You are twenty-five years old and have twenty-nine teeth, three shirts and eight socks, some books you no longer read, some records you no longer listen to" [24].) On first reading lines like these, it is almost impossible to entirely ignore, bracket, or erase the deictic function of the word "you" as it occurs in virtually every other discursive situation, where it refers invariably and exclusively to the addressee—that is, us. The implicit disparity (we are not twenty-five and have more or less than twenty-nine teeth) is then juxtaposed with a probable identity: in all likelihood, we possess several books we no longer read and, at the time of its publication, most readers would have had some records they no longer played. A continuous dialectic of identification and distancing ensues, as the reader is alternately drawn closer to and further away from the protagonist. This you is inherently unstable, constantly threatening to merge with the narratee, a character, the reader, or even with another grammatical person.

Historically, earlier theorists of narrative either ignored this kind of narration or dismissed it as a curiosity. Others claimed it clearly was a thinly disguised version of one of the two basic categories of narration. But which one? For Genette, this "rare and simple case" is readily situated as heterodiegetic narration (*Revisited* 133). Brian McHale likewise believes that "*you* stands in for the third-person pronoun of the fictional character, functioning in a kind of displaced free indirect discourse" (*Postmodernist* 223). Franz Stanzel takes the opposite position: despite his emphasis on the importance of the differences between first and third person narratives (80–83), he nevertheless contends that in "the novel in the second person . . . the 'you' is really a self-dramatization of the 'I,' and the form of the monologue prevails here, too" (225). He does confess in a footnote, however, that its "classification in my opposition of first-person and third-person form would cause difficulty if one did not consider it a variant of the first-person form, albeit a very significant one" (258). Matt DelConte likewise suggests that nearly "all second person narration is actually homodiegesis considering that a narrator must be on the same diegetic plane as his/her narratee-protagonist . . . in order to communicate with that narratee-protagonist" (210).

At this point we need to look closely at a few representative passages to help determine this issue. Many sentences in *La Modification* (the object of both Stanzel's and McHale's remarks) cannot be reduced to the first person. The book's second sentence includes the lines: "votre valise couverte de granuleux cuir sombre couleur d'epaisse bouteille, votre valise assez petite d'homme habitue aux longs voyages, vous l'arrachez" (9) ("you lift up your suitcase of bottle-green grained leather, the smallish suitcase of a man used to making long journeys" [1]); it is very difficult to imagine a veteran salesman muttering these words to himself, and in the formal, rather than informal, second person form at that, no matter how hard a day he's had. When Frenchmen speak to themselves, they always say "tu."[3]

On the other hand, this kind of narration cannot always be neatly subsumed under the rubric of the third person, so assiduous is it in depicting the stream of impressions, thoughts, and subverbal speech of the protagonist, as McInerney's *Bright Lights, Big City* reveals. The same is largely true of *Aura,* as its opening sentence discloses: "Lees ese anuncio: una oferta de esa naturaleza no se hace todos los dias. . . . Distraido, dejas que la ceniza del cigarro caiga dentro de la taza de te" (2) ("You're reading the advertisement: an offer like this isn't made every day. . . . You don't even notice when the ash from your cigarette falls into the cup of tea . . ." [3]). Here we are given both the protagonist's subvocal speech *and* the description of an event that he did not witness. It is in fact precisely this irreducible oscillation between first and third person narration that is typical of second person texts, texts that simultaneously invite and preclude identification with the other pronominal voices. Helmut Bonheim, who has argued for the even more constrained definition of narrative "you" as simultaneously designating the narrator, protagonist, and listener/reader of a second person text, nevertheless admits some of the more curious implications of this practice: "if one tells a story to a particular person who was on the scene of action himself, the reader will naturally ask why the 'you' needs to be told what he must already know" (76). In such cases, we may well conclude that that "you" is by this very fact *not* the narratee.

The ambiguity and fluctuation of this pronominal form are wonderfully captured by W. S. Merwin in a passage quoted by McHale,

> You are the second person.
>
> You look around for someone else to be the second person. But there is no one else. Even if there were someone else there they could not be you. . . . You make a pathetic effort to disguise yourself in all the affectations of the third person, but you know it is no use. The third person is no one. A convention. . . . No, you insist, it is all a mistake, I am the first person. But you know how unsatisfactory that is. And how seldom it is true. (116–17)

The second person is a playful form, original, transgressive, and illuminating, that is always conscious of its unusual own status and often disguises itself, playing on the boundaries of other narrative voices. This can be seen best by looking at the pronominal manipulation of the second person texts that most closely resemble first person narratives (*Bright Lights, Big City*) and third person novels (*A Pagan Place*).

In the first paragraph of McInerney's book we encounter the lines:

> You are at a nightclub talking to a girl with a shaved head. The club is either Heartbreak or the Lizard Lounge. All might come clear if you could just slip into the bathroom and do a little more Bolivian Marching Powder. Then again, it might not. A small voice inside you insists that this epidemic lack of clarity is a result of too much of that already. (1)

All of these sentences—and, for that matter, almost all of the sentences in the book—could be seamlessly transferred into the first person. Unlike the passage from *Aura,* they do not contain any information the protagonist is unaware of; unlike the quotation from Butor, they do not employ syntactic patterns alien to his customary discursive range. Nevertheless, the employment of the pronoun "you" brings with it an element of instability, of the very absence of clarity that is explicitly thematized within the passage. This effect is compounded by the mention of still another voice, the "small voice inside," that further fragments the protagonist's subjectivity. A number of hypotheses appear, ready to attempt to explain this curious situation: a psychomachia between self and soul, a dialogue between id and superego, a character employing the voice of another to interrogate himself, a realistic dramatization of the disorienting effect of cocaine. It is the nature of the second person narration to render all of these hypotheses plausible, while ensuring that no one can be definitive. As the novel continues, the interpretive possibilities decrease, though more playful deployments of narrative voices appear.

In the book's third chapter, entitled "The Utility of Fiction," the protagonist reads through a form letter sent by an insurance company to the female model that has recently left him. The letter reads: "Modelling is an exciting and rewarding career. In all likelihood, you have many years of earning ahead of you. But where would you be in the event of a disfiguring accident?" (37). Here, the fatuous prose and vulgar "you" of advertising copy—a ridiculous attempt to personalize a letter mailed to tens of thousands of potential customers—is surrounded by the narrative's considerably more subtle use of the second person.[4] The reader is presumably invited to consider the political implications of this juxtaposition. Is McInerney here satirizing commodity capitalism and attempting to subvert the advertising industry's possession of the "you" which, in the United States, is quite pronounced ("wouldn't you really rather have a Buick?"), or is it the protagonist's discourse that is infected by the discourse of the salesman, just as his thoughts are contaminated by tabloid headlines ("COMA BABY SIS PLEADS: SAVE MY LITTLE BROTHER," 11)?

A further twist appears when the protagonist remembers the more hopeful days of the recent past when he first applied for the job at the prestigious magazine that currently employs him:

> Already you feel a sense of nostalgia as you walk down the narrow halls past all the closed doors. You remember how you felt when you passed this way for your first interview. . . . You thought of yourself in the third person: "*He arrived for his first interview in a navy blue blazer. He was interviewed for a position in the Department of Factual Verification* . . ." (34)

In this passage, a rather ordinary perception, thinking of oneself in the third person, is entirely transformed when articulated in second person narration. A powerful effect of "defamiliarization" is achieved, as the unremarkable thought is teasingly framed by the unusual narrative mode.

A somewhat similar situation arises later in the novel when the protagonist speculates on issues of intersubjectivity:

> They're trying to imagine themselves in your shoes, but it would be a tough thing to do. Last night Vicky was talking about the ineffability of inner experience. . . . She said that certain facts are accessible only from one point of view—the point of view of the creature who experiences them. You think she meant that the only shoes we can ever wear are our own. Meg can't imagine what it's like for you to be you, she can only imagine herself being you. (101)

This passage discusses incommensurable viewpoints even as it plays with point of view. It chronicles the motif of the inability to communicate one's most profound feelings, one's "inner essence," even to those that are closest to one. (Significantly, the protagonist is not sure he grasps the precise meaning of Vicky's statement of the impossibility of fully conveying such meanings.) We may note that this paragraph, if written in the first person, would sound rather ordinary; its second person form, on the other hand, both invites an identification, however tenuous, between the protagonist and the reader, and introjects a ludic element of self-consciousness that makes the theme less bland. Furthermore, the one phrase in the novel that at first glance seems to betray the artificiality of the second person address, that makes it appear a gratuitous and even clumsy way to be original at any cost: "Meg can't imagine what it's like for you to be you," turns out, once the rest of the sentence is added, "she can only imagine herself being you," to yield a rather witty observation. The limits of Meg's consciousness are perfectly revealed.

In Edna O'Brien's *A Pagan Place,* the status and identity of voice and person are veiled in ambiguity at the beginning of the text. A recapitulation of a plausible reader response will disclose how the narration suggests different possibilities before finally revealing itself. The novel opens in the third person: "Manny Parker was a botanist, out in all weathers, lived with his sister that ran the sweetshop, they ate meat on Fridays, they were Protestants" (9). The next sentence, however, introduces the second person pronoun, and thereby raises the question of the status of the narrative and the identity of the speaker: "Your mother dealt there, found them honest." The next paragraph reverts to the third person until, several sentences later, "your mother" is referred to again. At this point, the customary assumption about the narrative transaction is, I presume, that we are in the presence of a "memory monologue"; some other older inhabitant of the village is narrating, without benefit of quotation marks, perhaps to an unidentified auditor. This reading is in turn problematized by certain odd locutions that seem more appropriately spoken by the ostensible narratee, who seems to be a child, rather than the presumed adult speaker: "When the cow did number two into the pail of milk, Mr. Wattle who was milking didn't see it" (10). This narrator, we might note in passing, employs a different ideolect from the voice that narrates elsewhere in the book, most prominently where unlikely objects of the child's knowledge are revealed:

> Your father met your mother at that dance but didn't throw two words to her. Your mother was all dolled up, home from America on holiday, had a long dress and peroxide in her hair. Your mother put the eye on

> him then and got her brother to invite him up to their house to walk the land. (12)

It is not until several pages later that we know with certainty that the person referred to as "you" is indeed the work's protagonist, and that the work is a standard second person narration, albeit an initially deceptive one. The "you" will continue to reach out to other perspectives; like all second person texts, this one continues to oscillate and merge with a number of other vantage points and usages, many of which David Herman has meticulously identified (337–68). The paragraph just quoted turns out to be not an eyewitness account but rather, it seems, the girl's personal version, one made up from other narratives, many of them no doubt frequently related within family circles, told (or rehearsed) to herself. The question then arises as to why O'Brien chose such an oblique and frankly misleading way of exfoliating her narration.

The answer is I believe a thematic one, and lies in the social world that surrounds and continually threatens to engulf the protagonist. She is a girl, possibly around the age of ten. Her family lives in poverty, surrounded by brutality: her parents quarrel cruelly, and her father is a violent alcoholic. As a girl, she is frightened and powerless in a highly stratified and harsh society. Virtually everyone she encounters, whether parent, priest, teacher, putative friend, or lewd stranger, erodes her selfhood and suppresses her speech. She internalizes this neglect, and acquiesces in her own silencing:

> She said there was nothing like bettering oneself. She addressed you but it was for your mother to register. Each time when you were on the point of saying something to Emma the words got caught in your throat and you could neither say them nor forget them and you could not utter them. You were like someone with a muzzle. (106)

Even in her own consciousness she views herself as a peripheral figure, a passive and largely inconsequential bystander. To refer to herself as an "I" would take more temerity than she possesses. Her subjectivity is muted, diffused, collapsed. Her "you" expresses her distance from her self.

Analogously, passages from Mavis Gallant's story, "With a Capital T," document the internalized debate of an independent female reporter writing under the conditions of wartime censorship: "At the back of your mind, because your mentors have placed it there, is an obstruction called 'the policy factor.' Your paper supports a political party. You try to discover what this party has to say . . ." (319). Once the narrator stops trying to accommodate the demands of her publishers, the narrative voice changes back to the "I" that began the tale. Here we see another way in which narration in the second person, in this case a change to and from the pronoun "you," enhances the representation of mental states.

An especially sustained and compelling juxtaposition of persons occurs in Nuruddin Farah's *Maps,* which will be discussed at greater length in the next chapter. Like Carlos Fuentes' *La Muerte de Artemio Cruz,* Farah's novel is written in alternating first, second, and third person sections, and the narrative perspectives differ in their depictions of the same protagonist: as Rhonda Cobham points out, the first person narrator is much more sympathetic to him than the second person narrator is (49). Farah plays as well with discontinuities in the second person form; the book begins with the sentence: "You sit, in contemplative posture, your features agonized and your expressions pained; you sit for hours and hours and hours, sleepless, looking into darkness, hearing a small snore coming from the room next to yours" (3). The first part of this sentence gives an external view of how the protagonist would appear to an observer; the rest of the sentence discloses perceptions that ordinarily would only be known to himself. This oscillation between internal and external perceptions that might normally be divided between first and third person narration or framed within a "limited omniscience" continues throughout the novel. Farah immediately goes on to add a metafictional twist to his narration:

> At times, when your uncle speaks about you, in your presence, referring to you in the third person and, on occasion, even taking the liberty of speaking on your behalf, you wonder if your existence is readily differentiable from creatures of fiction whom habit has taught one to talk of as if they were one's closest of friends. (3)

Later in the novel, in a particularly cunning move, Farah opposes the "we" of the authorial aside to the "you" of standard second person narrative: "Since we've been going backwards and forwards in time, let's continue doing so. But let us, for a while at any rate, spend some time with you, know how you were when you first came into their lives. . . . Your eyes said one thing to them, your silence another. And Hilaal and Salaado decided to wait, placing themselves between these aspects of yourself (as Hilaal put it), knowing full well there was another you" (138). Here a distinct narrator addresses the protagonist rhetorically before moving on to a more standard description, and then goes on to record the possibility of another, hidden "you" behind that standard "you." Taken together, these features make *Maps* one of the most powerful displays of the importance of the distinction of person and the richness of second person narrative in contemporary literature.

In summary, we may observe that the choice of the "you" form radically alters the tone of the work and provides a unique speaking situation for the narrator, one that does not occur in natural narratives and consequently one that continuously defamiliarizes the narrative act. Its usage can engender a heightened engagement between reader and protagonist in different directions: we may oppose identification with a "you" we resist, or we may sympathize more fully with a central character like McCarthy's: "Now and then, this look of commendation would rest particularly on you; whenever this happened, it was as if, in his delight, he had reached over and squeezed you" (149). Or, as often occurs, a dialectic is established in which the reader alternates between identification and distancing. The technique simultaneously opens up new possibilities for representing consciousness and provides a site for the contestation of constricting discursive practices. Of most importance for traditional narrative theory, second person narration is situated between but irreducible to the standard dyads of either first and third person or hetero- and homodiegetic narration, but rather oscillates irregularly from one pole to the other. As Fludernik affirms: "second-person fiction destroys the easy assumption of the traditional dichotomous structures which the standard narratological models have proposed, especially the distinction between homo- and heterodiegetic narrative (Genette) or that of the identity or nonidentity of the realms of existence between narrator and characters (Stanzel)" ("*Natural*" 226). We may now turn to the other two modes of second person narrative, modes that cannot be simply converted to the first or third person

II. The Hypothetical Form

Lorrie Moore's *Self-Help* is a collection of daring short stories, most of them in the second person. These differ from what I have termed the "standard" mode; as many of their titles suggest ("How to Become a Writer," "How to Be an Other Woman," "The Kid's Guide to Divorce"), they are written in the style of the user's manual or self-help guide. I originally called this mode "subjunctive"; other rubrics such as "hypothetical" or even "recipe form" now appear to be in wider use. This technique goes back at least as far as what Morrisette ("You" 11) terms the "pseudo-guidebook" style of the opening pages of Robert Penn Warren's 1946 novel, *All the King's Men;* it has been used in a number of recent stories, including John Updike's "How to Love America and Leave It at the Same Time" (1979), Margaret Atwood's "Happy Endings" (1983), and Pam Houston's "How to Talk to a Hunter" (1990). A few sentences from Moore's story "How" will disclose some of the idiosyncratic features of this mode:

> Begin by meeting him in a class, in a bar, at a rummage sale. Maybe he teaches sixth grade. Manages a hardware store. Foreman at a carton factory. He will be a good dancer. He will have perfectly cut hair. He will laugh at your jokes. . . . [F]rom time to time you will gaze at his face or his hands and want nothing but him. You will feel passing waves of dependency, devotion, and sentimentality. A week, a month, a year, and he has become your family. (55)

Here we find three features generally absent from standard second person narration: the consistent use of the imperative, the frequent employment of the future tense, and the unambiguous distinction between the narrator and the narratee.[5] The protagonist is a possible future version of the narratee, though it soon takes on an independent, parallel existence. Equally noteworthy are the unspecified and virtually arbitrary natures of the male character, the setting, and the chronology of events. These elements are not, however, entirely gratuitous. There is a certain plausibility about the locations of the first meeting and of the time period customary for passion to unfold. As to the man's occupation, the extreme degree of specificity—not merely a teacher or store manager, but a sixth grade teacher or a hardware store manager—is rather incongruous, unexpected, and amusing: a single woman does not usually go to a bar with such precise expectations. The foreman of the carton factory at first glance strains the sense of probability and is clearly intended as a comic element, and yet on further reflection this figure can be read as one of the inescapable improbabilities in life that sooner or later inevitably appear. What Moore provides, in short, is a kind of enumeration and interrogation of the typical, identifying the remotely possible as well as the more likely scenarios.

Ironically, this very wealth of possibility gradually gives way to a strange kind of necessity; the protagonist is unable to be happy with any man, whatever his occupation. ("Back at home, days later, feel cranky and tired. Sit on the couch and tell him he's stupid. . . . He will try to kiss you. Turn your head. Feel suffocated" [57]). The stories almost always end sadly; they are a caustic parody of the glowing self-help manuals they pretend to imitate. The plots chart the succession of poor decisions, casual betrayals, and unavoidable tragedies that life invariably provides, instead of the delusory fictions happily proffered by paperback psychologists.

It is worth observing that many non-literary books employing this form of the second person are often highly gender coded. Fix-it manuals, especially those dealing with gasoline engines, are regularly directed to a very male reader; most recipe books and many self-help volumes specifically target a female audience. The narrative audience reader of the stories that compose *Self-Help* is usually female; consequently, it may not be inaccurate to see these stories as, in part, a feminist critique of an extra-literary genre that ultimately preys on the female readership it purports to serve.

The "hypothetical you" is also a protean one, perhaps even more so than the "you" of standard second person texts, which can occasion some ontological slippage. As James Phelan observes, at the ending of "How," "narratee, ideal narrative audience, and narrative audience all nod their heads in understanding here. The close positioning of the complementary audiences strengthens the second-person's general invitation for the narrative, authorial, and actual audiences to project themselves into the narratee's position" ("How" 362). This "you" is one that can embrace almost all of us.

III. The Autotelic Form

The defining criterion of my third category, "the autotelic," is the direct address to a "you" that is at times the actual reader of the text and whose story is juxtaposed to and can merge with the characters of the fiction. It is a narrativization of a form of address, and as such appears in relatively "pure" instances only in extremely short texts, such as Merwin's "The Second Person." In more extended works, it alternates with third or first person narration. This mode may first have originated in Lautréamont's *Les Chants du Maldoror,* is present in Beckett's *The Unnamable* ("You wouldn't think it was the same old gang as a moment ago, or would you? What can you expect, they don't know who they are either" [372]). This form is most thoroughly deployed at the beginning of Italo Calvino's *Se una notte d'inverno un viaggiatore*. Like the "hypothetical" form, it plays with the construction of the typical, and the narrator is quite distinct from the narratee. Like standard second person fiction, it is told primarily in the present tense, and some pronominal shifting is evident. Its unique and most compelling feature, however, is the ever-shifting referent of the "you" that is continuously addressed. Calvino's novel opens with descriptions of the reader interacting with the book, "You are about to begin reading Italo Calvino's new novel, *If on a winter's night a traveller*" (1). This sentence necessarily applies to every actual reader who starts the volume at the beginning. Here description is reenactment; the reader's response is portrayed even as it is being created. The narrator's present tense is identical to the temporality of its reception. As John T. Kirby explains, "In McInerney's narrative, the reader knows that he or she is extradiegetic, outside the narrative, and only assumes identity with the main character as part of the act of play in which reading consists. Calvino's sophisticated strategy is to catch you, the extradiegetic reader, off guard, and make you the subject of diegesis, thereby spiriting or abducting you into the narrative" (11).

Calvino's text goes on to give advice concerning its consumption:

> Find the most comfortable position: seated, stretched out, curled up, or lying flat. Flat on your back, on your side, on your stomach. In an easy chair, on the sofa, in the rocker, the deck chair, on the hassock. In the hammock, if you have a hammock. On top of your bed, of course, or in the bed. You can even stand on your hands, head down, in the yoga position. With the book upside down, naturally. (1)

Here, Calvino designates the most likely settings that the reader has already just chosen. With the exception of this slight temporal gap, the "you" of the text continues to correspond with the actual reader of the book, except in the unlikely event that one is, say, reading the passage while standing in the office of the foreman of the carton factory. A kind of game now begins; as long as Calvino accurately depicts our physical position or mental response, he is addressing the actual reader in an uncomfortably proximate manner. Once he slips, digresses, or changes tack, however, as he does when he describes the reader struggling to open the packaging that envelops the book—an act that cannot occur simultaneously with our reading a depiction of it—we return to the more familiar role of the conventional reader: the "you" now designates a fictional character, one who is merely a dramatized narratee. Throughout the text the "you" continues to move, shift, double back, and change again, addressing alternately the real reader and the narratee.

In another passage, Calvino writes: "So here you are now, ready to attack the first lines of the first page" (9). This is directed to the narratee, since the actual reader has begun the novel several pages earlier. Calvino continues: "You prepare to recognize the unmistakeable tone of the author. No. You don't recognize it at all. But now that you think about it, who ever said this author had an unmistakeable tone?" These lines too are addressed to a narratee; the implied reader has already perceived the Calvino touch—the sly irony, the undermining of narrative conventions, the relentless reflexivity. The author now raises the stakes: "On the contrary, he is known as an author who changes greatly from one book to the next. And in these changes you recognize him as yourself." The actual reader will probably concur with the first of these statements, while the implied reader will see in the second sentence another version of the theme of identity—of individuals, of narrative situations, and of the book itself—that permeates the text. When Calvino goes on to observe, "Perhaps at first you feel a bit lost" (9), the locution may simultaneously refer to all the different readers (narratee, implied, and actual) that traditional narratology attempts to keep separate in theory as well as a character called the Reader (see Margolin, "You" 441–42). At the same time, it both alludes to and enacts the anti-essentialist stances concerning personal identity characteristic of poststructuralist theory and postmodern narrative. In this work, literature and theory interanimate each other, the concept of person dissolves, and presentation fuses with representation.

Looking back over these three basic types of second person narration, we may clarify the nature of each by contrasting which figures are juxtaposed, fused, or destabilized. "Standard" second person narration oscillates between third and first person perspectives, with each narrative usually settling toward one or the other, while repeatedly if briefly seeming to include the reader as the object of the discourse. Hypothetical second person texts fuse a heterodiegetic depiction of an ever more specific individual with an imagined future of the reader, thus merging a third person perspective with a hypothetical "you" that is the virtual equivalent of "one." Autotelic texts have the greatest share of direct address to the actual reader and superimpose this onto a fictional character designated by "you" that tends to be treated from an external perspective as if in the third person. This intensifies one of the most fascinating features of second person narrative: the way the narrative "you" is alternately opposed to and fused with the reader—both the constructed and the actual reader.

All "you's" are not equal, however, and not everyone is equally able to merge with the second person. After all, as Brian McHale points out, "Italian grammar forces Calvino to specify the number and gender of his Reader in the original text—the Reader is, at the outset, masculine, singular" (*Postmodernist* 256), though by the end he has two readers, one male, the other female, go off together.[6] A comparable point is made forcefully in Jamaica Kincaid's nonfictional book on Antigua, *A Small Place,* a work that takes its discursive tone from another variety of second person writing, the travel guide:

> You disembark from your plane. You go through customs. Since you are a tourist, a North American or European—to be frank, white—and not an Antiguan black returning to Antigua from Europe or North America with cardboard boxes of much needed cheap clothes and food for relatives, you move through customs swiftly, you move through customs with ease. Your bags are not searched. (4–5)

By identifying the racial and economic status of her "you," Kincaid reveals the dynamics of the divided audience, and challenges the monolithic "you" that implies a universal, deracinated, ideal construct. Kincaid is painfully aware of antithetical communities of reception, as well as the ideological codes that typically surround notions like the ideal reader. The assumptions that white middle and upper class audiences bring to the act of reading are thus foregrounded and exposed—particularly the insidious assumption that they are, "naturally," the universal you addressed by the text. As the book's frequent reflections on language make clear ("For isn't it odd that the only language I have to speak of this crime is the language of the criminal?" [31]), Kincaid's interrogation of the "you" is part of a larger critique of imperialists' objectifications of colonized peoples. In this context, one is reminded of another poignant usage of the second person that also addresses a divided readership—the final words of Ralph Ellison's *Invisible Man:* "what else could I do? What else but try to tell you what was really happening when your eyes were looking through? And it is this which frightens me: Who knows but that, on the lower frequencies, I speak for you?" (568). This passage, with its rhetorical questions, internal rhyme, and direct address, easily evokes the rich oral tradition of African-American storytelling, a tradition that stresses interaction between speaker and audience. Once again, we see that by identifying and contesting an already appropriated "you," minority writers are better able to create a discursive space where their own voices may be heard.

Performed narratives can also employ this technique, though the fact that the "you" is spoken alters its effects. An audience in the theater can be addressed by an actor or a character in a play. The following speech opens Athol Fugard's play, *My Children! My Africa!* "You've got to drive in first gear all the time because of the potholes and stones. . . . I think you'd be inclined to agree with our mayor" (15). A more radical address to the spectators and narrative of the audience's behavior appears in Peter Handke's "Insulting the Audience."

While first person cinema has been widely discussed by theorists like Edward Branigan, George Wilson, and Sarah Kozloff, second person film is rarely mentioned (although here too Morrissette offers some interesting commentary: "You" 20–21). There is no question that second person films do exist; military forces routinely employ them for training new recruits. But cinema lacks the immediacy of the theater where actors can directly address individual spectators;[7] its mode of production and reception makes any attempt to speak to its viewers something of a gamble. More significantly, the existing conventions of narrative film militate against second person narrative cinema. Edward Branigan observes that characters are prohibited from staring into the camera in the classic film in order to preserve the spectator's status as invisible voyeur (46). When it does occur, direct second person address is generally coded as a personal narration that reveals the subjectivity of the speaker. Branigan concludes that we may speak of "unmotivated" camera movement and direct address to the camera only because a standard of neutral narration and reception exists. In every film text, he affirms, there must always be "an underlying level of omniscient narration—that which frames but is not itself framed—and voyeuristic reception—that which looks but is not itself seen—which together create the fictional appearance of other levels of narration" (46). This may help to explain why, in the film version of *Bright Lights, Big City,* the second person narration was invariably perceived as the voice of the protagonist speaking to himself. One might add that this situation need not always be the case, as the beginning of Lars von Trier's film *Zentropa* demonstrates. Its second person voiceover was so compelling that some film critics could not resist writing their reviews in the second person.

§

It is easy to guess why narrative theory has resisted conceptualizing second person fiction for so long. There is of course the force of habit, especially the habit of thinking in terms of binary oppositions. For those theorists attempting to construct a universal narratology, capable of embracing all narratives, both factual and fictional, an additional problem appears: first and third person novels have obvious nonfictional counterparts in autobiography and biography, but second person narrative is an exclusively and distinctively literary phenomenon, its only nonfictional analogues being the pseudo-narrative forms of the cookbook, the travel guide, and the self-help manual. The typical discourse of the standard second person novel ("The newspaper—it was folded to the listings of single rooms—fell from your pocket when you drank from the bottle," [Hawkes, 5]) has no precise nonfictional equivalent. Here, a thorough poetics of fiction as actually practiced in the twentieth century will threaten the dream of a universal narratology, a situation that I will discuss at greater length in the conclusion to this book.

One may now assess the distinctive characteristics of second person narrative. First of all, it is a relatively novel mode of narration, one that allows innovative authors a fresh way to treat traditional fictional situations, and one that permits authors to explore the boundaries of and invent variations on a new fictional voice, as many of the authors discussed above amply demonstrate. It may even turn out to be one of the most important technical advances in fictional narration since the introduction of the stream of consciousness. Though second person narration seems peculiarly suited to the concerns of postmodernism, it is important to observe that numerous other aesthetic stances have found the strategy fruitful: romanticism (Hawthorne), expressionism (Aichinger), magical realism (Fuentes), realism (O'Brien), and high modernism (Butor).

Secondly, it offers new possibilities of creative representation, particularly for revealing a mind in flux. The narrative "you" is especially effective in disclosing the sense of intimate unfamiliarity present in the cocaine-charged brain of McInerney's anti-hero, in the dream-like self of Fuentes' Felipe Montero throughout his mythopoetic adventures, and in Aichinger's protagonist's journey through death and time. The narrative "you" is also admirably suited to indicate the suppressed subjectivity and silenced speech of O'Brien's female protagonist, and one might also suggest that Butor's "*vous*" is peculiarly appropriate for describing the mind of a conflicted individual in the process of making significant decisions that he would prefer not to have to think about. And, in a very different way, Calvino impressively documents the act of reading even as it is taking place.

The ideological possibilities of second person narration are also rich. It invites a rewriting of commercial discourses intended to exploit their readers through the illusion of identification, it helps dramatize the mental battles of a individual struggling against the internalized discourse of an oppressive authority, and it is a useful vehicle for minority writers to foreground a subjectivity typically excluded from common, unexamined notions of "you" and "us." And at a more philosophical level, it is admirably suited to express the unstable nature and intersubjective constitution of the self.

Class and Consciousness

"WE" NARRATION FROM CONRAD TO POSTCOLONIAL FICTION

chapter three

An examination of second person fiction might appropriately be followed by an account of the other major new form of telling a story: "we" narration. From certain perspectives, however, the two types seem quite different. Unlike second person narratives that are "unnatural" from the outset—that is, that do not exist in "natural narrative"—first person plural texts are typically directed to a much wider audience and do not immediately call attention to themselves as artificial constructs possible only in literature. However, we will see that literary "we" narratives routinely (if at times barely perceptibly) make themselves strange and likewise produce unlikely or impossible kinds of telling. "We" narration, a common strategy in contemporary fiction, also has a relatively long though little known history that extends for over a century. Many works in this mode are insistently intertextual, carrying on a number of conversations among each other and with other discourses. Their dialogism is further manifested in the ways in which first person plural narration often appears in juxtaposition to other modes of narrating. Apart from a few notable studies, those of Morris, Lanser (*Fictions* 239–66), Woller, Britton, and Margolin ("Telling," "Collective"), it has been largely unexplored in the theory of narration and was essentially unrecognized before 1992. In this chapter I will discuss the unexpected origin of this practice in Joseph Conrad's 1899 novel, *The Nigger of the 'Narcissus,'* and trace the way this strategy works as opposed (and juxtaposed) to other modes of narration as well as how it participates in another significant innovation: multiperson narration. I also trace the varied ideological work the narration performs as it depicts the crew's oscillation between isolated individualism and a more collective consciousness.

Using a chronicle form that indicates causal connections as well as independent story strands, I will go on to reconstruct the subsequent history of this technique, noting the very different ideological uses to which it has been put and the varied models of subjectivity it presupposes. Throughout, I will focus on a few central, recurring issues, the first of which is, Who constitutes the narrative's "we"? The first usage of "we" in John Barth's *Sabbatical* is accompanied by a footnote which reassuringly states that the identity of the people that form the "we" will soon be disclosed. Barth here is formally (and facetiously) articulating a convention of "we" narration: virtually no first person plural narrative discloses its membership at the outset; there is always a bit of drama as the reader determines just who this "we" is.[1] The beginning of Mark Helprin's "North Light" begins with the nonspecific line, "We are being held back" (4), moves on to a description of the ridge "we" occupy and the valley below, a depiction of natural forms that does not give any precise information about the setting, neither which continent they are on nor which century it is. It is then made clear that there is a war going on, and that "we" are soldiers. Finally, it is clarified that the "we" represents a group of Israeli soldiers in tanks waiting to attack Syrian forces in the 1973 war.

"We" may represent an intimate or a vast group, and its composition may—and usually does—change during the course of the fiction.[2] Uri Margolin further points out (1996) that it occupies "an intermediate position between the sender role (I) and those of the second and third persons (not-I)" ("Telling" 117); that is, the speaker necessarily speaks in the name of him- or herself and of another. Another important question is how homogeneous or disparate the "we" cluster is, and how it becomes more or less inclusive as the text progresses. The "we" form also raises interesting issues concerning reliability: insofar as it is a subjective form, it is enmeshed in issues of reliability and discordance, but these are issues that are potentially different from those in first person singular narratives since they may involve more accurate intersubjective beliefs as well as communal misprisions or even mass delusion. Finally, we will note how instances of "we" narration interact with adjacent forms (especially first person singular and third person) that so often accompany them.

A first person narrator who frequently uses the plural pronoun to denote the action of a group is not unknown in earlier fiction; Aphra Behn's narrator in *Orinooko* often employs it to designate the white colonists in Surinam. The narratives I am concerned with below differ insofar as they produce a tension concerning the identity and knowledge claimed by the "we" voice. More to the point, Susan S. Lanser has documented what might be called the prehistory of "we" narration in two nineteenth century works that employ an "I" narrator yet express a collective subjectivity: Elizabeth Gaskell's *Cranford* (1853) and Sarah Orne Jewett's *The Country of the Pointed Firs* (1896). Lanser notes, "These 'singular' communal narrators are constructed through subtle but important departures from autodiegetic practices, for while the narrators retain the syntax of 'first person' narrative, their texts avoid the markers of individuality that characterize personal voice and thereby resist the equation of narrator and protagonist. Rather, the narrator's identity becomes communal" (*Fictions* 241). The most relevant antecedent, however, is certainly the opening paragraphs of *Madame Bovary* (1857) in which a "we" speaker narrates the introduction of Charles Bovary into the boys' classroom before seamlessly if mysteriously yielding to the discourse of the primary narrator and vanishing from the text.

In *The Nigger of the 'Narcissus,'* Conrad's use of "we" narration begins deceptively as the work opens in the conventional manner of standard third person narrative. Other than the brief comment that the mate, Mr. Baker, "kept all our noses to the grindstone" (31), the work continues in the third person until a common bond begins to appear among the seamen and "we" becomes the privileged perspective: "We hesitated between pity and mistrust" (36); "We spoke in low tones" (37), and so on. That is to say, Conrad uses different modes of narration in counterpoint to the consciousness of the men he is depicting. The greater their cohesion, the more insistent the use of "we"; a bond is likewise established between the narrator and the crew. Later in the voyage, as sailors retreat back into their own individual selves, the classic third person form returns.

"We" in this text refers to most of the crew, the men of the forecastle as opposed to the officers. It does not usually extend to include the malcontent Donkin, the West Indian James Wait, or Singleton, who represents an earlier generation and, as boatswain, ranks slightly higher than the crew proper. Thus, the seamen's perceptions of Donkin are represented in terms that express difference: "He stood on the bad eminence of a general dislike. . . . Our sea-boots, our oilskin coats, our well-filled sea-chests, were to him so many causes for bitter meditation: he had none of these things, and he felt instinctively that no man, when the need arose, would offer to share them with him" (40). Intriguingly, in this passage the "we" narrator discloses the contents of Donkin's mind, something of course a first person narrator, singular or plural, is not supposed to be able to do.

As noted above, "we" narrators can attain a highly probable intersubjective sense of things or they can produce an unreliable narration that is bounded by the epistemological limitations of the group they belong to. Conrad takes care to utilize the full range of these options, producing a number of observations that are both technically innovative and resonate with the effect of the real. Similar or shared thoughts are depicted as if they were part of a single mind. This practice, however, grows more odd and less realistic the longer it continues, as can be seen in the progression in the following passages: "We were appalled. We perceived that after all Singleton's answer meant nothing. We began to hate him for making fun of us. All our certitudes were going. . . . We suspected Jimmy, one another, and even our very selves" (43). Especially ironic is the claim that we suspected each other, since each individual is entirely in unison in distrusting the others. Elsewhere, what might be called "group unreliability" strikes: the crew is convinced that Wait's desire aided by Wamibo's presumed magic spells "delayed the ship in the open seas. Only lubberly fools couldn't see it" (142). At other times, the unreliability becomes self-conscious and openly acknowledged: "we . . . sympathised with all [Wait's] repulsions, shrinkings, evasions, delusions" (139). That is to say, the "we" perspective affirms what it wishes to believe even when it knows it is mistaken.

Conrad returns to third person narration at a few points in the novella to achieve a particular thematic point; in doing so he enacts a miniature drama of the use of narrative perspective. Thus, in the third chapter, as a storm hits the ship, the men's cohesion begins to break down and the voice of the narrator returns to the third person, using "they" to refer to the men (48–50). The narration, that is, dramatizes the men's retreat from a shared consciousness as the storm thrusts them back into their isolated selves: "Huddled close to one another, they fancied themselves utterly alone. They heard sustained loud noises, and again bore the pain of existence through long hours of profound silence" (82).[3]

Later in the text, Conrad transforms his narration again. A deluded "we" consciousness appears that is fueled by the malignant Donkin's usage of a rhetorical "we," as he employs the language of socialist agitation to incite the crew to mutiny: "He told us we were good men—a 'bloomin' condemned lot of good men.' Who thanked us? Who took any notice of our wrongs?" (100). This period of collective false consciousness (99–103) is followed by extended third person passages, as if Conrad were dramatizing the selfishness and egoism leading up to the mutiny, signaling it as a perverted kind of union. Suggestively, the ensuing mutiny itself is mostly depicted in a literally depersonalized manner, as acts are committed by unidentified agents: "In the shadows of the fore rigging a dark mass stamped, eddied, advanced, retreated. There were words of reproach, encouragement, unbelief, execration" (122). As the passive voice continues, the action is scattered and further depersonalized: "A lot of disputes seemed to be going on all round"; "The hurling flight of some heavy object was heard" (123). The ineffectual mutiny dissolves the men's common bond of labor and replaces it with a fragmenting and confused discourse. Once order is restored, the "they" narration takes control, as Conrad counters the existing "we" narration of socialists and revolutionaries with an antithetical model of group consciousness which stems from a collective sense of duty.

In the final chapter, the ship gets closer to home and the narration returns to the "we" form. The "we" voice speaks for the final time as the *Narcissus* comes into its port (166). Once on land, "they" narration is used to depict the men in their last moments together in the shipping office where they are paid off. But in the final paragraphs of the novel, Conrad introduces his final, concluding transformation, as an "I" narrator suddenly irrupts in the text and continues the story seamlessly: "Charley and Belfast wandered off alone. As I came up I saw a . . . woman . . . fall on Charley's neck" (170). The narrator goes off by himself, with nothing but his pay, his memories, and an isolated consciousness.

Conrad anticipates many subsequent uses of voice and narration that would not become widely used until fairly recently. We may identify three distinct achievements in this work: 1) the first sustained example of "we" narration, 2) a rare early text that effectively employs multiperson narration, alternating between first person plural and third person narration, and also using the first person singular and passive voice narration at strategic points in the text. Most daring, however, is 3) the transcendence of the strictures of realism in the alternation of the "we" and "they" segments, since the "we" voice cannot know the private thoughts of many of the seamen disclosed by the third person narration. More audaciously, the two voices are not clearly separated and often glide into each other. This juxtaposition of mutually exclusive narrative stances can be seen prominently in passages where a sentence of "we" narration is followed in the next line by a third person plural account: "Our little world went on its curved and unswerving path carrying a discontented and aspiring population. They found comfort of a gloomy kind in an interminable and conscientious analysis of their unappreciated worth" (103). From the perspective of a mimetic theory of narration, the speaker either is or is not part of the group and therefore one of the pronouns is misleading. Other examples are even more resistant to a realistic recuperation. As many Conrad critics have pointed out, the entry into the consciousness of Singleton, Wait, and others is incompatible with the narrator's claims of having performed physical action onboard: "Groaning, we dug our fingers in, and very much hurt, shook our hands, scattering nails and drops of blood" (68). If the narrator is a character on the ship, he cannot enter the minds of others or report conversations he has not observed; if he is omniscient, he can't break fingernails onboard, but only pare them silently, from a distant vantage point far above his creation. The narrator, that is, is simultaneously homodiegetic and heterodiegetic.[4]

Conrad criticism has, quite understandably, found this intercalation of voices to be problematic; scholars do not even agree on how many narrators the book has.[5] The difficulty with such critical approaches is that they presuppose an exclusively mimetic conception of the narrator; that is, they can only imagine him as one (or two) human being(s) who writes only what an individual consciousness is likely to know or a traditional omniscient mind is expected to reveal. Conrad is doing something much more radical here, something that transcends the mimetic poetics that such criticism implicitly presupposes.[6] There is no single, self-consistent discursive subject in the text. We need to ask, "What is the narration doing now?" rather than, "Who is speaking here?" By following out the varied narrative voices, however, we find that they themselves constitute a kind of narrative that complements and underscores the central events and ideas of the story.

Conrad provides theoretical support for the kind of reading I have offered in his preface to the work: to show life in all its vibration, its color, its form, the artist "cannot be faithful to the temporary formulas of his craft," including those of "Realism, Romanticism, [or] Naturalism" (xiv–xv). It is precisely the mimetic conventions of realism that

Conrad transcends in this work as he creates a different discourse situation that cannot be found in actual human communication. In doing so, I suggest he anticipates the more extreme abrogations of mimesis in late modernist and postmodern texts discussed elsewhere in this book.

In the history of narrative technique after Conrad, we find many of the same concerns reappearing in different guises. Henri Barbuse's *Feu*, a 1916 novel about World War I, is mostly narrated in the "we" form, and is stridently opposed to the war it depicts. It explicitly discusses the unusual nature of the individuals that have come to form its collective subject: "Despite all the variations in age, origin, education and status, and everything that used to be, despite the gulfs that used to divide us, broadly speaking we're the same. Behind the same crude shape we conceal and exhibit the same manners, the same habits, the same simplified character of men who have reverted to their primal state" (18). This text also plays with the precise constitution of its "we": most of the time, it refers to the individuals that form the patrol, at other times it refers to the entire battalion, and at a few moments it embraces all soldiers.

One is particularly struck by the intensely political uses the technique is routinely put to. The next significant occurrence of "we" narration appears in Yevgeny Zamyatin's cacotopian novel, *We*. Written in 1920–21, it was not allowed to be published in Russia because of its critique of the excesses of Soviet authoritarianism, millenarianism, and scientism, and on the new state's ruthless insistence on obedience and conformity. A staunch Bolshevik for many years, Zamyatin was disgusted to see the revolution he had helped create degenerate into the very tyranny Conrad had predicted would ensue. This work was first published in an English translation in 1924, and its unauthorized appearance in a Russian émigré publication in 1927 brought about his denunciation by and consequent resignation from the Soviet Writers' Union. This futuristic novel opens as the narrator is praising the state and its collectivist mentality, which he attempts to merge with his individual self: "I shall merely attempt to record what I see and think, or, to be more exact, what we think (precisely so—we, and let this *We* be the title of my record)" (4). Collective descriptions are first provided in "we" form; as the novel develops, it is rapidly replaced by an "I" that is increasing dissatisfied with the status quo. The few "we" usages here are primarily markers of indoctrination and servility; the protagonist is most honest and authentic when he says "I."

An opposite response was provided by Victor Serge, another early Communist supporter and early critic of the new Soviet state. With Zinoviev, he helped form the Communist International; by 1923, however, he had joined the Left (Trotskyist) Opposition; in 1928 he was expelled from the party and arrested. He wrote his major works of fiction at this time, sending them to France for publication since their printing was forbidden in the Soviet Union. His main novel, *Naissance de notre force,* an account of the anarcho-syndicalist uprising in Barcelona in 1917, was published in Paris in 1931. Its first chapter and its final segments employ the first person plural; in between an "I" narrator (who often speaks for a larger group of revolutionaries) is the primary voice. In discussing his choice of pronouns, Serge articulated sentiments that would continue to be expressed by many subsequent practitioners of this form: "The word 'I' is repellent to me as a vain affirmation of the self which contains a large measure of illusion and another of vanity or unjustified pride" (1977: 15). Appropriately, Serge's subject is the collective struggles and emotions of the men who attempt to overthrow the egoistic economic and cultural world of capitalism.

In Italy Ignazio Silone, a founding member of the Italian Communist party, wrote the anti-fascist novel *Fontamara* in exile in Switzerland in 1930. It would first appear in print in a German translation three years later. It became extremely popular, selling a million and a half copies and appearing in twenty-seven languages as the struggle against fascism spread around the world. When Allied troops occupied Italy, the U.S. Army printed an unauthorized edition of the book and distributed copies to Italians in the areas they had liberated. The novel uses a "we" voice throughout, in large part as a naturalistic method of indicating the collective sensibility of the Fontamara peasants. Their life is shared, and so is their story. The "we" refers to the villagers of Fontamara (as distinct from the residents of the nearby town); occasionally, it fails to include two or three of the most wayward of the village's inhabitants.

As the novel progresses, readers of the work in Italian soon perceive that the narrator is female through the use of gendered adjectives. The speaker then briefly refers to herself as "I" ("Michele Zompa and I stopped at the table" [17]) before returning to her customary "we" narration; much later, we learn her name (30). In the third chapter, the "we" voice continues speaking ("There was bitterness in our hearts . . . with our soup plates on our knees, we talked about nothing else" [55]). This time the narration is differently gendered, however; these words are spoken by a man who later is abruptly revealed to be the husband of the first speaker (59). Husband and wife alternate speaking in the next few chapters, at one point yielding to the eyewitness testimony of the other ("My husband can tell you the rest if he wants to" [101]). It is as if discrete individuals (and even their age, temperament, and gender) are relatively unimportant; the same narration could be expected from most any of the villagers.

Further in the narrative, the speaker of the "we" changes again as the transmission of the story is passed on to the couple's son, who narrates the eighth and ninth chapters. The setting alters: the son and one of the more rebellious of the villagers go to town and take the train to Rome, the communal sensibility melts away, and the "we" narration ceases. Instead we get a standard first person account of the two men's journey; a typical sentence reads, "He seemed to need to go on talking, so I let him" (146). That is, the shared consciousness does not appear to extend beyond the social space that produced it. In the final chapter, the son returns to the village and helps radicalize the others there, and the "we" narration is briefly reestablished. By printing an oppositional newspaper the peasants quickly bring down the wrath of the Fascist authorities, who attack the village and decimate the people. The father, mother, and son, who were on the road when the assault began, then flee to Switzerland.

Use of "we" narration serves to depict the radical disjunction between the perceptions of the peasants and those of the more urban residents. Each group is profoundly ignorant of the world of the other, and has no clue how it functions or what its rules are. What is obvious to one group is inconceivable to the other. At times, the peasants are presented as almost farcically innocent of modern bureaucratic society; elsewhere they are shown to have a sagacity that entirely eludes their urban coevals. Throughout the text, the "we" sensibility is presented as an excellent medium for a communal consciousness and as the basis for collective action. The need for continued and increased social unity is thematized within the text; at one point the villagers speculate on their relative powerlessness before the Fascist enforcers and attribute their weakness to a basic egoism: "Physically, each one of us was a match for at least three of them. But what link did we have in common? . . . We were all born at Fontamara, and here we were all together in the village square; that was what we *cafoni* had in common, and that was all. Apart from that, everyone thought of himself" (103). What is needed is still stronger group unity and consciousness.

As we will see, a substantial number of colonial and postcolonial authors have gone on to use the "we" form of narration to express their struggles against the imperial powers. The first is Raja Rao's *Kanthapura* (1938), which depicts the arrival of Gandhi's independence movement in a village in South India and is in some senses an Indian reconfiguring of some of Silone's themes and techniques. (Rao acknowledged Silone's novel as the inspiration for his own.) The primary narrator is an old woman who conveys the communal sensibility through the constant use of the pronouns "we" and "us" but never strays into the territory of an omniscient voice.[7] The "we" here is more delimited, and generally includes only some portion of the adult members of the South Indian village, minus the large landowners and the Dalits, or "untouchables." At times her "we" only designates women; at other times, it includes only Brahmins.[8]

She communalizes (and subjectivizes) knowledge of the world beyond the villages by prefacing it with the words "they say," itself a partially indeterminate form that exists on the border of third person narration. This results in an unusual epistemic status, the articulation of "what is known," which is situated somewhere between the invariably idiosyncratic subjectivity of a single individual and the necessarily objective account of a standard third person narration. As first person narration becomes increasingly eccentric in twentieth century fiction and omniscient third person narration seems increasingly inauthentic, "we" narration appears as an intersubjective correction that nevertheless eschews omniscience. As we saw in Conrad, "we" narration can vary in its reliability, being less dependable at times, and more so at others. In the case of Kanthapura's narrator, she is both ill-informed and partially untrustworthy at many points in the text. Recounting the mythological account of the coloration of the hill, she states that the goddess Kenchamma waged a battle with a demon whose blood soaked into the earth: "Tell me, how could this happen if it were not for Kenchamma and her battle?" (2). Elsewhere in the novel, however, she appears to have more detailed knowledge than she should realistically be able to acquire, and the novel has been faulted on these grounds. It is precisely Rao's attempt to conform to a realistic epistemology that prevents him from utilizing much of the playfulness, defamiliarization, and innovation that other practitioners have extracted from this technique. For our purposes, the key point is the inclusiveness and flexibility of the subjects depicted in this fashion. And, as the narrative continues and villagers unite in a common struggle, the "we" designates a collective subject that becomes both more specific and more heterogenous.

William Faulkner uses "we" narration in a number of ways in his short fiction. Most common is the case of a first person narrator recounting the experience of a small group or members of a family, as "That Evening Sun" records the shared feelings of the Compson children, a technique that would also be used much later by Toni Morrison in *The Bluest Eye* (1970). Faulkner's story is especially compelling in its depiction of the utter incommensurability of the world of the secure white children and that of the threatened black woman; the "we" here marks an unbridgeable social and hermeneutic divide. A more daring example is Faulkner's ultimately unsuccessful attempt to use a "we" to speak for the Other, as Native Americans "voice" their collective impressions in "A Courtship." Most significant for our critical and theoretical purposes are the more capacious "we" narrations in stories like "A Rose for Emily," which utilizes a rural voice that speaks for the higher class of white males. The story begins with a relatively unobtrusive collective pronoun ("When Miss Emily Grierson died, our whole town went to her funeral" [119]) which quickly dissolves into third person narration but then resumes with a number of interesting "we" statements. At one point, it is averred that "we" sent her a tax notice (128). It is not entirely correct to assume that here the "we" refers to the members of the municipal government, as Margolin avers ("Telling" 120). Instead, it seems to me the "we" represents a much larger collective, and continues to refer to the better-off members of the community. This synecdochic "we" becomes even more compressed elsewhere in the story, where what would normally be the perception of a single individual is presented as a shared experience: "When we next saw Miss Emily, she had grown fat and her hair was turning gray" (127). This surely is a kind of first person plural way of saying "the next time she was seen in public. . . ." By the end of the story the collective "we" does change and becomes an actor, physically present in the story: "For a long while we just stood there . . ." (130); now the "we" has narrowed and been made concrete, as did Raja Rao's, from the town in general to a smaller group of particular individuals acting and feeling in unison in a specific time and place.

A more striking and sustained use of "we" narration appears in the work of yet another disillusioned Communist: Richard Wright's

12 Million Black Voices (1941), a photobook made in collaboration with photographer Edwin Rosskam. As Joel Woller has remarked, the first chapter "is narrated in a cross-generational voice. . . . It functions as a kind of prologue, articulating a collective memory of the middle passage and slavery" (348). In a paragraph describing the horrors of the middle passage, the iterative narration includes the experiences of both the living and the dead: "In the summer, down in the suffocating depths of those ships, on an eight- or ten-week voyage, we would go crazed for lack of air and water, and in the morning the crew of the ship would discover many of us dead" (14). The next chapters are narrated in the present rather than the past tense; according to Woller, the collective voice of the second chapter is rural, southern, and parental; the third chapter is youthful, proletarianized, and urban; while the final chapter takes on a prophetic tone and brings the "dynamic we-you dialectic" (348) to its conclusion, thereby producing the most daring expansion of the composition of the "we": "The differences between black folk and white folk are not blood or color, and the ties that bind us are deeper than those that separate us. . . . Look at us and you will know yourselves, for *we* are *you,* looking back at you from the dark mirror of our lives" (146).

It will not come as a surprise that the experimental techniques employed by practitioners of "magic realism" include the use of first person plural narration. Julio Corázar presents an obsessed group of movie fanatics in "We Love Glenda So Much" (1981); for the purposes of this book, the most compelling is the unusual narration in Mario Vargas Llosa's "The Cubs" ("Los cachorros" [1967]). In this text, "we" and "they" forms alternate, not merely in successive sections or passages, but within the same sentence: "Todavia llevaban pantalón corto ese año, aún no fumábamos, entre los deportes preferían el fútbol y estábamos apriendo a correr olas . . ." (107) ("They were still wearing short pants that year, we weren't smoking yet, of all the sports they liked football best and we were learning to ride the waves . . ." [1]). As Jean O'Bryan-Knight comments, "in a single sentence . . . we observe the group [of four boys] subjectively and objectively" (340). Vargas Llosa has thus compressed the epistemological antinomy devised by Conrad into a starkly unnatural form, thereby foregrounding the transgression that "we" narration always threatens to enact: the collapsing of the boundary between the first and the third persons. O'Bryan-Knight goes on to suggest that the use of this strategy has ethical implications: "A powerful consequence of this complex perspective for us as readers is that we are simultaneously made to identify with the members of this group and to pass judgement on the group as outsiders" (340, cf. 343–45).

Postcolonial writers, following Raja Rao, have found the first person plural form to be an especially fitting technique to embody a number of shared concerns. Ngugi wa Thiong'o, who, like Faulkner, was an assiduous reader of Conrad, employs "we" narration in a short chapter at a central node of his novel, *A Grain of Wheat* (1967). The most important political and social event, the arrival of Kenyan independence, is narrated by a brief, abrupt, and most Conradian foray into the first person plural: "His name was on everybody's lips. We wove new legends around his name and imagined deeds. We hoped that Mugo would come out and join us" (204). This affirmation of narrative presence is emblematic of a unity between characters, implied author, and authorial audience, rather than a verisimilar depiction of a group of people who were literally there. Ayi Kwei Armah also uses "we" narration throughout his novel, *Two Thousand Seasons* (1973). His "we" is a term of resistance, and is repeatedly opposed to the inaccurate discourse of a "they," as we see from the beginning of the first chapter: "We are not a people of yesterday. Do they ask how many single seasons we have flowed from our beginnings till now? We shall point them to the proper beginning of their counting" (1). Here "we" explicitly designates several overlapping groups of past and present Africans and people of African descent. This produces some compelling features, including a collective memory which is set forth as authoritative: "Our clearest remembrances begin with a home before we came near the desert of the falling sun" (4). A major drama of the book is the failure of the disparate groups to fully converge; as Margolin observes, "the source of Africa's tragedy, according to Armah, is the unbridgeable gap between the People of the Way [contemporary African political activists] and the rest" ("Collective" 125). This technique of narration is well suited to presenting an alternative group's aspirations and sensibility, as we have already seen; it would be used again to present a comparable postcolonial critique by black writers from the Caribbean and South Africa.

Martinican Edouard Glissant has written three novels that employ "we" narration: *Malemort* (1975), *La Case du commandeur* (1981), and *Mahagony* (1987) and has called for a "roman de nous" to adequately express the Antillean experience and sensibility. In *Caribbean Discourse* (1989) he states: "The author must become demythified, certainly, because he must be integrated into a common resolve. The collective 'We' becomes the site of a generative system, and the true subject" (149). Dawn Fulton (2003) explains this stance further: "For him the idea of Martinican identity cannot be thought in the singular, but only in the plural, and only in a manner that works with 'relation,' of connections and conflicts between and among individuals" (1105) Within the novels themselves, she goes on to note, Glissant acknowledges the difficulties of establishing a collective voice that is able to tell a single story convincingly and authentically (1108). Appropriately, these novels will later go on to produce an intertextual rejoinder in Martinican Patrick Chamoiseau's 1997 "we" novel, *L'Esclave vieil homme et le molosse,* as the "we" form continues to be insistently dialogical.[9]

The vast majority of "we" texts valorize collective identity in no uncertain terms; "we" is almost always a favored term and a desirable subject position that is to be sought out and inhabited. Pierre Silvain's 1971 novel, *Les Eoliennes,* uses the "we" form to produce an opposite effect as it resuscitates and extends the trope originally set forth by Zamyatin. Silvain's novel is written entirely in the first person plural about a cluster of technicians, each devoid of any individuality. Margolin explains: "Having lived and worked together for so long, they perform a large number of tasks . . . in a perfectly co-ordinated manner. . . . But the joint actions they perform, physical and mental, are by and large routine and trivial. . . . The resultant impression is that of a group of largely de-individualized, depersonalized agents, an autonomous uniformity of near clones performing a series of predetermined, senseless routines" ("Telling" 128). The first person plural represents a powerful trap that the characters are unable to escape. In this regard, it looks ahead to some of the narratives of the 1990s that rethink the larger implications of this narrative form.

Gynocentric fiction has, not surprisingly, utilized the "we" form along the lines of other groups advocating collective action to redress social grievances. Joan Chase's novel, *During the Reign of the Queen of Persia* (1983), is a narrative about three generations of women, all descended from a matriarch, who live together on a farm in Ohio. In this text, the "we" refers to the granddaughters; variations in the specific individuals designated by the pronoun only serve to confirm the shared interests and sensibilities of all: "There were four of us—Celia and Jenny, who were sisters, Anne and Kate, sisters too, like our mothers, who were sisters" (48). Variations in the specific individuals designated by the pronoun only serve to confirm the shared interests and sensibilities of all. In what could be a partial summary of this narrative technique, the text states: "Sometimes we watched each other, knew differences. But most of the time it was as though the four of us were one and we lived in days that gathered into one stream of time, undifferentiated and communal" (48).

Adalaide Morris observes that "in any number, in any combination, at all moments, they speak only in the first-person plural. Although they fight viciously among themselves, these girls are 'sisterhood' incarnate" (20); the use of this technique creates a "fused 'we' of sisterhood" (25). The situation is in fact still more complex: the "we" applies only to the sisters as a collective entity; when any individual girl is discussed, the third person form is used exclusively. That is, in ordinary discourse, "we" implies a single speaker that is part of the group; this narrator, however, never refers to any of the girls as "I" even though she must be one of those four if the conventions of mimesis are being followed. In a work that otherwise closely adheres to realistic conventions, it can be disorienting to have to conclude that one of the women must be speaking of herself in the third person, a situation for which there is normally no realistic justification. Thus we return to kind of mimetic paradoxes displayed by Conrad, as an otherwise scrupulous realism is transcended by innovative techniques of narration.

Hertha D. Sweet Wong has analyzed collective speaking subjects in traditional and recent Native American women's autobiography. She notes that "a Native autobiographer, whether a speaking or a writing subject, often implies, if not announces, the first person plural—we—even when speaking in the first person singular. 'We' often invokes *a* (sometimes *the*) Native community" (171).[10] She also notes that contemporary Native American writers use the technique in a less literal manner, gesturing toward a larger community that is invoked rather than depicted by the pronoun. Two comparable tendencies can be found in Louise Erdrich's novel, *Tracks* (1988). This book alternates between the narratives of the tribal elder, Nanapush, and that of the younger, mixed blood Pauline. The old man's narrative frequently uses the "we" form, and it may expand out to include the spirits of the dead or else contract to refer, Faulkner-like, merely to the small group he is traveling with at the time.[11] Pauline's narrative is almost entirely first person singular with only a few usages of a fairly conventional plural form. This pattern of alternation itself depicts the move away from a traditional, collective sensibility rooted in the land to a more isolated, individuated, and mobile existence that interacts with the encroaching world of the white people. Another feminist use of "we" appears rather dramatically in Julia Alvarez's 1991 novel, *How the Garcia Girls Lost Their Accents.* The first portion of the text is presented in third person narration and the last portion is in the first person. At the center is a crucial chapter that employs "we" narration; it describes first the shared lives of the sisters and then the strategy employed to prevent the youngest from marrying a controlling, sexist man. In this section, the "we" of solidarity that is lost by Erdrich's speakers is partially recovered by Alvarez's.

A different "we" novel of this period uses its narration to demonstrate an inability to identify with a group of women. Jeffrey Eugenides' *The Virgin Suicides* (1993) "we" narrator is a partially indeterminate collection of neighborhood boys who, despite years of investigation and speculation, never begin to understand the motives of the girls who kill themselves. This novel includes a number of subtle, self-reflexive allusions to the idea of a multiple, protean subject. Looking at the youngest girl's diary, the boys learn that "Celia writes of her sisters and herself as a single entity. It's often difficult to tell which sister she's talking about, and many strange sentences conjure in the reader's mind an image of a mythical creature with ten legs and five heads, lying in bed eating junk food, or suffering visits from affectionate aunts" (42). This is not a bad description of a common effect of "we" narration, and captures one of its uncanny features. This passage is followed by another that remarks on another standard practice of this kind of narration concerning the depiction of a shared consciousness: reading the diary together, "we learned about their lives, came to hold collective experiences of times we hadn't experienced, harbored private images of Lux leaning over the side of a ship to stroke her first whale" (42–43). Here Eugenides provides a partial, naturalistic explanation for one of the more original and unnerving features of such prose, intended perhaps for those made uneasy by the nonrealistic aspects of "we" narration.

Interestingly, in the film version of this work directed by Sofia Coppola (1999), the more unusual features of Eugenides' "we" narration are absent: the voice-over is performed by a single male speaker, making it seem like one of Faulkner's more ordinary short stories in which a single character narrates events that happened to himself and two or three companions. Likewise, visual images of four boys sitting down looking at Celia's diary preclude any play with the precise identity and extent of the group. Finally, the "reality effect" of the images on screen tends to overwhelm and minimize the narrating that frames them, a phenomenon that has been noted by many film theorists. Looking back at Faulkner's "That Evening Sun" or Armah's *A Thousand Seasons* as well as the gynocentric texts just discussed, we may conclude that "we" narration is equally effective in portraying one group's inability to comprehend another as it is in forging understanding between disparate individuals. It may either bridge or ossify difference.

Four recent works demonstrate both the staying power of the form and the range of innovations it remains capable of: Nathalie Sarraute's *Tu ne t'aimes pas* (1989), Zakes Mda's *Ways of Dying* (1995), Joyce Carol Oates's *Broke Heart Blues* (1999), and Hazard Adams's *Many Pretty Toys* (1999). These might be summarized as, respectively, a postmodern psychomachia; a Shandean investigation of postcolonial uses of the "we"; the presentation of different, overlapping, fallible group consciousnesses; and a metafictional commentary on the fragmented communal subject. The larger trajectory that all four trace is a further subjectivizing of the "we," as its hitherto stable, intersubjective function gives way to unreliable group sensibilities.

Nathalie Sarraute's first novel, *Portrait d'un inconnu* (1948) inaugurated a kind of experimental novel that would later be called the *nouveau roman*. In all of her fiction she explores subvocalized speech, preverbal impulses, unspoken sentiments, and the constant negotiation of a private, fragmented self with a shifting and derisive "they" composed of external voices. *Tu ne t'aimes pas* (1989, translated the following year as *You Don't Love Yourself*) is a representation of a collection of contiguous voices, some of them contradictory, that seem to form a single, decentered consciousness. Here, the instabilities that flavor nearly all "we" narration are mapped onto the voices of a deconstructed self. As one of the voices complains at the outset of the book: "Of course, we were a little restless, a little ill at ease, embarrassed . . . Not all of us, though . . . We never turn out in full force . . . there are always some of us who are dozing, lazing, relaxing, wandering . . . this 'we' can only refer to the ones who were there when you came out with that remark" (2, Sarraute's ellipses). The work is not so much a psychological study as a philosophical allegory of the multiple subjectivities and voices bound together in a self, as the unstable, shifting, and always incomplete "we" voices provide an apposite image of this polydirectional entity.

Oates' novel proceeds rather simply if cynically. *Broke Heart Blues* is narrated by a succession of different, overlapping groups using the first person plural: girls attending the high school, the younger women of the town, the sons of the wealthy, the boys attending the high school, and so on. Each narration centers on the figure of John Reddy Heart, a high school student who is arrested for killing a man. The different voices share a similar melodramatic sensibility and sensationalistic vocabulary that quickly blend together into what might be described as a single, bubble-gum voice, though one that often includes ironic commentary on collective subjects:

> We laughed but were thinking the identical thought. If our parents knew. If guys at school knew. Shelby Connor said, "*He* wouldn't tell." Millicent LeRoux said, "That isn't the point. The point is, we've got our pride. Dignity. We are who we are. I mean—aren't we?"
>
> "No! No! No!"—we squealed like maniacs. (6)

As the discursive differences between the groups disappear, Heart takes on quasi-mythic status in the shallow minds of his peers. What results is a narration of multiple "we's" that all sound depressingly similar and reveal the impoverished imaginations of the speakers.

Hazard Adams' novel has rather less material in first person plural than the other texts discussed here, but it develops the notion of the unreliable "we" further and takes it in new directions as it further problematizes the identity of its collective subject. *Many Pretty Toys* is set during the sixties, and every third chapter of the novel is told by a "we" voice. Adams reproduces the multiple, divided, and contradictory components of this most disunified subject more thoroughly than any earlier writer other than Sarraute; intriguingly, this voice possesses an insistently metafictional sensibility, and suspects it (they) may be directed by another, greater power. Both of these aspects, the scrupulously precise and the extravagantly postmodern, are linked together in numerous passages: "And so we begin, except that we can also be regarded as having begun, or even eternally telling our tale. Some of us claim, of course, that the tale is really ours, that we have invented it in order to speak a piece we can lay claim to. Some of us point out that if the author spoke before we began, it is possible that those words of his are spoken after ours as well as during or before. Whether or not this means he or He should not be trusted is debated among us" (18). As the novel progresses, "we" find themselves in a situation analogous *both* to that of the disgruntled characters in the novel within the novel in *At Swim-Two-Birds* and to Borges' most ontologically suspicious personae. Much of the drama of the "we" sections is its attempt to determine the nature of this author figure and thus better understand their own destinies.

Zakes Mda provides the most playful and sustained interrogation of the curious epistemology of the "we" narrator; an early passage in *Ways of Dying* reads as if it were intended to answer critics of the practice of Conrad and many of his successors:

> We know everything about everybody. We even know things that happen when we are not there; things that happen behind people's closed doors deep in the middle of the night. We are the all-seeing eye of the village gossip. When in our orature the storyteller begins the story, "They say it once happened . . .," we are the "they." (12)

In an attempt to ground the impossible knowledge of the contents of other minds in a first person form, the speaker playfully locates the source of such knowledge in a more unreliable (yet widely believed) source, the village gossip, and then goes on to associate this narration with the wellspring of traditional oral literature. The speaker continues with some salient reflections on the control and selection of narratives in this kind of speech community and a direct address to a potentially skeptical audience: "No individual owns any story. The community is the owner of the story, and can tell it the way it deems fit. We would not be needing to justify the communal voice that tells this story if you had not wondered how we became so omniscient" (12). Here we have a slyly ironic and politically charged explanation (or pseudo-explanation) for information not available under a rigorously mimetic framework. Together, these four recent novels show the richness and vitality of the "we" form and suggest that its potential for further development remains quite promising.[12]

§

In Uri Margolin's most recent statement on the subject, he has suggested that "we" narratives are rare for three related reasons: because the exact scope of the "we" may remain ambiguous and may contain different members at different points in the narrative, because the question of the narrators' access of others' minds "remains inherently unresolved," and because the sense of a collective subject is more easily conveyed in lyric or meditative texts ("Collective" 253). The examples above, I would argue, suggest a different conclusion on all three charges. "We" narration is instead a supple technique with a continuous history of over a century that continues to be deployed in a considerable number of texts, particularly those that emphasize the construction and maintenance of a powerful collective identity, including feminist and postcolonial works.[13] It has been utilized by a considerable number of major twentieth century authors as well as significant figures prominent in oppositional literatures. It is the very ambiguity and fluctuations of the precise identity of the "we" that are among its most interesting, dramatic, and appealing features, and most apposite for an age that eschews fixed essences. "We" narration is especially effective in juxtaposition to other, traditional modes of narrating. This results in a distinctive kind of multiperson narration that continuously defamiliarizes the conventional nature of traditional narrative forms.

It is certainly the case that it is an excellent vehicle for expressing a collective consciousness; the relative rarity of its use heightens its ability to highlight traditional formulas and foreground its difference from the autonomous individual consciousness associated with the rise of the novel in England and the development of modernist techniques of representing minds. For socialists, feminists, and Third World intellectuals who denounce the extremes of bourgeois egoism and the poverty of an isolated subjectivity, "we" narration must seem a prefiguration of the new, more communal, and more egalitarian society they are working to promote. The form is also singularly adept in providing expression of the shared sensibilities of a number of different groups, including Conrad's seamen whose lives may depend on each man performing his tasks; the isolated rural communities of Silone, Rao, and Faulkner and the pre-industrial *Gemeinschaft* they share; the circle of revolutionaries of Ngugi and Armah; the segregated urban poor of Morrison or Mda; the soldiers of Barbusse and Helprin; the children's sensibility depicted by Faulkner and Vargas Llosa; and the crass cliques portrayed by Oates. Perhaps most impressively is its repeated use by black Africans and members of the African diaspora (Wright, Ngugi, Armah, Glissant, Morrison, Mda, Chamoiseau) all of them as it were rewriting, revising, or signifyin' on *The Nigger of the 'Narcissus'* as the story of that text's unassimilable Other is told and retold in the technique Conrad invented.

Concerning Margolin's second objection, we may agree that the narrator's access to the contents of other minds is potentially problematic, but hasten to point out that this is only an issue if we insist on postulating a mimetic framework for the text. If one ignores these parameters, as Conrad does, or gives them a postmodern wink, as Mda prefers, then the "problem" dissolves. Further, as Adams demonstrates, a precise if occasionally schematic designation of the exact beliefs of each differing subgroup is also possible in this format. In a different way, Butor provides a mimetically plausible depiction of the thoughts of disparate members of a crowd at a railway station in "La Gare St. Lazare." Finally, in the case of Glissant's *La Case du commandeur,* this very oscillation can be effectively thematized within the text. As Celia Britton observes, the novel opens and closes with direct references to the problem of building a collective identity; its final sentence concludes: "We, who so impatiently gather together these disjointed I's [*ces mois disjoint*], determined to contain the anxiety of each body within this difficult darkness of us [*cette obscurité difficile de nous*]" (Britten, 140).

Even within a realistic framework, it is not clear to me that the presumed knowledge of other minds is always some kind of embarrassment. Margolin explains: "any 'we' mental action description [inevitably combines] first person inside knowledge with a second- or third person inferential one. The fact that the 'we' is not an authorized spokesman for [the group] makes this problem more acute" (253). But is this charge true of a simple claim such as that predicated of Conrad's seamen when they are first confronted with Wait's claim that he was mortally ill: "we hesitated between pity and disgust" (36)? This is surely a wide enough spectrum to include each individual's belief. More extravagant claims are equally innocent: "We suspected Jimmy, one another, and even our very selves" (43). This statement is presumably a shortened form of "Many (or most) of us suspected Jimmy, others suspected one another, some even suspected themselves"—again, a perfectly reasonable contraction. Finally, consider the case of a statement of a shared perception that is literally false: "We were afraid he would fall in and kill one of us" (69). Though all may have been concerned about the situation, it is obvious that only a few (at most) would have had that specific thought. The point of this kind of narration is not that a meaningless accuracy has been attempted and has failed, as an interview with each character about his state of consciousness at the time would reveal. Instead, Conrad's statement captures an important aspect of the sensibility of the crew and certainly reveals the thought of at least one of its representative members. Rather than an inherently flawed technique, it seems to me to be instead an extremely flexible strategy that works precisely because of its variable referents. The drama created for the reader is thus to determine how literally and how figuratively to take each such expression of shared mental events. The "we" glides between the lone individual and the entire collective;

between a strict and a more lax denotation; and between mental experiences that are entirely, partially, or minimally shared.

It is most useful to see the "we" narrator as a different kind of figure from the realistic type of first person narrator and more like a postmodern first person narrator who is not bound by the epistemological rules of realism.[14] I argue that "we" is an essentially dialectical perspective that typically (and most successfully) plays with its own boundaries. As Celia Britton observes, "its extreme elasticity provides a point of view that is not limited to any one character or period of time but moves around from one to another. . . . As such it creates a different representation of intersubjective relations between the individual characters, suggesting that people's most intimate feelings are known to the community" (142). Much of the drama of reading such a work comes from observing the fluctuations in the group that constitutes the "we," assessing its explicit epistemological statements concerning the origin and veracity of its beliefs, attending to moves away from realism and toward a more paradoxical discourse, and noting fundamental changes in the general reliability of the "we" narrator.

Indeed, one of the great challenges of reading this kind of fiction is to establish the relative objectivity or subjectivity of the "we." One may even discern a general, if intermittent, historical trajectory that moves from more reliably intersubjective narrators earlier in the century to ever more unreliable ones and then back again to a playful, postmodern "communal omniscience." The "we" narrators of Silone, Rao, Wright, and (most of the time) Conrad, when confined within their own spheres of experience, are utterly reliable. Those of Eugenides and Oates are utterly fallible, while Glissant and Mda self-consciously provide their narrators the authoritative knowledge they should not normally be able to possess. The "we" of Wright and Erdrich can even include the voices of the dead. To this one may add another important function that leads directly to the subject of the next chapter: the suggestive interplay between "we" narration and more conventional first and third person forms. In such texts, the "we" discourse is propelled into prominence, alternates suggestively with other perspectives, or is even left behind once its thematic and narratological functions are completed.

To return once more to the question of the politics of narration that keeps recurring in discussions of all the innovative modes of narration discussed so far in this book, we may observe that the vast majority of works mentioned in this chapter have a definite and often insistent political agenda; the "we" form seems to attract revolutionaries of all stripes, even more so than the "you" narratives discussed in the previous chapter. With "we" texts, however, the narration may take on completely antithetical valences. This token of progressive self-awareness and group consciousness from Silone to Mda is also the mark of servility, blindness, and oblivion in Zamyatin and Silvain. The canny method of revealing the sagacity of indigenous, plebian or rural groups can equally well depict small town stupidity and hysteria. Conrad's means of honoring the seamen who knew and performed their duty is also the term by which we know the genuine socialist revolutionary in the anti- and postcolonial texts. Given the range of positions the form has been used to set forth, we may safely conclude that there is no inherent ideological valence in any narrative form, despite the vigorous claims of its various champions.

The chronicle form I have employed in this chapter, though lacking the dynamism of narrative proper, is nevertheless well suited to indicate the many direct and indirect connections or convergences among different narrative traditions over the past century. A number of obvious lines of descent immediately present themselves: *The Nigger of the 'Narcissus'* was one of Faulkner's favorite books, Faulkner was carefully studied by Wright and Morrison and was considered by Vargas Llosa to be the paradigm of modern novelists; Ngugi is a keen reader of Conrad and a novelist widely read by later postcolonial authors; Rao admitted he derived this technique from Silone; and so forth.

If we look at these texts synchronically, we may determine other correspondences as well. An inventory of the most salient varieties of "we" narration, differentiated according to the degree to which they diverge from the poetics of realism, could be aligned as follows: 1) Conventional: the unproblematic case of a single narrator describing events experienced by him- or herself and others, as found in Faulkner's simpler "we" stories, such as "That Evening Sun." Technically, this is not really a "we" narration as I use the term above, but a first person singular narration that includes reference to others. 2) Standard: largely realistic narration that nevertheless stretches verisimilitude at key points, especially when the narrator discloses the inner thoughts or feelings of a group or when, as in Joan Chase's novel, the "we" voice of shared experience and the third person accounts of each girl's individual actions cannot be realistically squared. This is by far the most common form, found from Silone and Serge to Eugenides and Oates. 3) Nonrealistic: in the texts by Conrad, Wright, Armah, and Mda we have flagrant violations of the parameters of realistic representation. Conrad's are done solemnly without remark and Mda's are self-consciously displayed; Wright's and Armah's narrators disclose sentiments that stretch over centuries and range across continents. 4) Anti-mimetic: the texts of Sarraute and Adams eschew realism altogether, and function instead as experimental constructions of multiple discourses that can inhabit a "we."

This minimal classification can also help us pinpoint the distinctive theoretical differences of "we" narration: whenever a text uses a first person plural narrator to depict the thoughts of others, it necessarily straddles the line between first and third person fiction, as a homodiegetic character narrator discloses that which can only be known by an external heterodiegetic intelligence. These narrations are thus simultaneously first *and* third person discourses, and transcend either subtly or flagrantly the foundational oppositions set forth in different ways by Stanzel and Genette.[15] Whereas most second person narration oscillates between these two poles, "we" narration curiously occupies both at once.

I, etcetera

MULTIPERSON NARRATION AND THE RANGE OF CONTEMPORARY NARRATORS

> It'll never be known how this has to be told, in the first person or the second, using the third person plural or continually inventing modes that will serve for nothing.
> —Cortázar, "Blow Up"

chapter four

Another of the more significant omissions in contemporary narrative theory is the absence of sustained accounts of multiple modes of narration. Thus, while many typologies contain a space for both Bloom's subvocal speech and Molly's internal monologue, there is usually no place in such schemas for *Ulysses* as a whole, as if the conjunction of different narrators and modes of narration was not itself of primary theoretical importance.[1] This gap is all the more unfortunate when one considers a work like *The Sound and the Fury,* in which the first person "memory monologues," as Dorrit Cohn calls them (*Transparent* 247–55), are starkly juxtaposed to the resolutely third person segment that concludes the novel. Still more compelling for readers and potentially problematic for theory are texts in which the same character's thoughts and actions are narrated in different persons, or when entirely disparate narrators converge. As such texts continue to proliferate, and the varieties of multiperson narration expand, it becomes all the more urgent to identify, analyze, and theorize this impressive group of texts. One of the consequences of this analysis is a reaffirmation of the significance of the distinction between first and third person narration (and homo- and heterodiegetic moods); if the previous two chapters show how these forms are often made to fuse, this chapter will underscore the importance of establishing and maintaining this distinction for twentieth-century novelists.

In what follows I will examine a number of different texts that employ multipersoned narration. Three major kinds of multiperson texts may be identified at the outset: works that move back and forth between different narrative positions, those whose narration remains fundamentally ambiguous, inclining toward but never comfortably situated within either category, and those strange texts that employ unnatural narrational stances that are impossible in nonfictional discourse. In addition, we might note another general opposition: "centripetal" texts that begin by producing a number of seemingly disparate voices and stances only to reduce them to a single narrating position at the end, and "centrifugal" texts that continue to proliferate an irreducible galaxy of different, heterogenous or antithetical, perspectives. Since many of the critics of the works I will be discussing frequently invoke ideological reasons to explain the author's chosen narrative practice, I will also briefly discuss claims concerning the politics of narrative person as I have done in the previous two chapters.

§

Alternating narration between different grammatical persons is not an exclusively modern phenomenon. As Stanzel has pointed out, Thackeray's narrator employs both "I" and "he" to describe his life in *Henry Esmond.* A historical survey of these practices will include other titles Stanzel discusses in this context: Conrad's *Under Western Eyes,* Robert Penn Warren's *All the King's Men,* Bellow's *Herzog,* and several novels by Max Frisch (104–10). To this group of course we may add the many texts that, following Conrad, juxtapose a "we" narration to a first person singular or a third person form. In *Bleak House,* an omniscient third person narrative is accompanied by the first person account of one of the characters. Discussing Dickens' novel, Stanzel explains that the "two narrative situations represent two different perspectives, namely, the panoramic one of the authorial narrator who is critical of the times, and the naive but sympathetic viewpoint of the first-person narrator, Esther Summerson, circumscribed by her domestic horizons" (71). Even in this description, it might be noted, we get a sense of the ideological valences present in such a gendered division of knowledge and narration. As Susan Sniader Lanser explains, by "replicating the ideology of separate spheres," *Bleak House* sets "the omniscient and implicitly male voice of the authorial narrator next to the personal voice of the female character Esther Summerson without acknowledging this duality" (*Fictions* 239–40).

Contemporary fiction is replete with a polyphony of competing narrative voices; even where the narrator's speaking situation seems fixed, alternative voices often threaten to destabilize that situation. A representative example of this kind of play with person can be found in Alberto Moravia's 1971 novel *Io e lui* (literally, *I and He* or *Ego and Id*), which dramatizes the battle between a man's reason and desire by having each presented in its appropriate person.[2] Texts like this effectively embody the intersubjective constitution of "the" self and the instability of the classical ego, and one can follow out the drama of identity as the libidinal "he" keeps attempting to include the resisting narrative "I" within a shared identity ("Enough of that plural. We are not 'we,' we are 'I' and 'you'" [8]). One can also find a more realistic though more ambiguous separation and conflation of person and voice in "Unguided Tour," the last story in Susan Sontag's collection, *I, etcetera* (1978), in which an apparent dialogue between an "I" and a "you," transcribed without quotation marks, is collapsed into other voices and texts.

Clarice Lispector's *Agua Viva* (1978) seems to be a missive from a woman to her lover, with "I" and "you" firmly locked in their conventional places. As the narrative continues, the "I" disintegrates: "I divide myself thousands of times, into as many times as the seconds that pass, fragmentary as I am" (4). While the speaking self is continuously dispersed and multiplied, the addressee expands to include the various readers of the text: "I write you completely whole and I feel a pleasure in being and my pleasure in you is abstract, like the instant" (4). These two pronouns and their elusive referents are soon further reconstructed, as the narrator announces that "if I say 'I,' it's because I don't say 'you,' or 'we,' or 'a person.' I'm limited to the humble act of self-personalization through reducing myself, but I am the 'you-are'" (6). Here, an act of apparent humility—not presuming to speak for someone else—is simultaneously disclosed to be a bold claim to do just that. And this occurs through the curious act of "self-personalization through reducing myself," a practice that superficially can seem either tautological or self-contradictory unless we recognize it as a persuasive statement of the intersubjective constitution of a fluid and multiform subjectivity.

Lispector's drama of person, self, and other continues as the narrator explains that she is "still not ready to speak of 'him' or 'her'" (28);

the introduction of the third person pronoun proper in the form of the story of João will not be presented until much later in the text (48). In the meantime, the narrator is transfixed by the pursuit of the "it," as in "I need to feel the *it* of the animals again" (38), that is, a kind of primordial sensibility beneath or beyond mere individuality: "it seems I'm achieving a higher plane of humanity. Or of inhumanity—the *it*" (43). At this point, other pronouns fuse: "You have become an I" (43). The work ends with a pseudo-classical resolution. The narrator, who began by asking "Who am I?" claims to have found herself, and in the process realizes the disjunctive corollary that, after all, "you are you" (79). But it is no longer clear exactly what these terms refer to after their conventional meanings have been so thoroughly effaced. The narrative practice of Lispector and others tends to elude conventional theoretical models because it implodes or transcends the stable, determinate identities presupposed by those theories.

The contemporary use of multiperson narration is marked by Nabokov's abrupt shift from "I" to "we" narration in the final chapter of *Speak, Memory,* originally published in 1951 as *Conclusive Evidence.* In narrative fiction, the systematic alternation of first and third person narration seems to begin with Elizabeth Jane Howard. Her 1959 novel, *The Sea Change,* consists of a series of alternating accounts of four individuals involved in the same web of events. The male playwright is the only one treated in the third person; his male attendant and his sickly wife employ first person memory monologues, and the naive young woman from the countryside is presented exclusively through her diary and letters home. Together, the figures present a compelling, dynamic picture of consciousnesses that either strive for an objective, public sensibility or withdraw into a safer, bounded subjectivity.

Recently, a number of novels have appeared that alternately use the first and the third person pronouns to designate the same character. A survey of some of these can establish what exactly is at stake in the deployment of multiple personal reference, both aesthetically and ideologically. The first chapter of Fay Weldon's *The Cloning of Joanna May* (1989) is narrated in the first person and is followed by three third person chapters; then the work returns to the first person for a chapter which is followed again by three more third person chapters. This pattern, with a few basic variations, continues throughout the novel. Since the first person account is that of a woman struggling to achieve a sense of self—and escape the depredations of the brutal patriarchal world that threatens first to marginalize and then to kill her, we may be forgiven if we first approach this work as another reinscription, pace Dickens, of the public (male)/private (female) hierarchy. In fact, however, a dual epistemology is presented in the text, one deterministic, materialistic, patriarchal, and murderous; the other more spiritual, communal, female, and alert to the play of chance. The ultimate triumph of Joanna May and her achievement of self, community, and survival—the victory, that is, of the "I" over the "he"—constitutes a rewriting and reversal of the very hierarchy inscribed by Dickens. Intriguingly, many of the novel's thematic oppositions are first expressed in terms of the second person:

> 'Love' I could understand, but what did he mean by this 'you'? Small children (so I'm told) start out by confusing 'me' with 'you.' Addressed so frequently as 'you,' their clever little minds work out that this must be their name. 'You cold,' they say, shivering, as the wind blows through the window. 'Not you,' comes the response, 'me.' 'Me cold,' says the child, obligingly. Presently the little thing progresses to the gracious 'I am cold.' But is the 'me,' the 'I,' really the same as the initial 'you' with which we all begin; the sudden bright consciousness of the self as something defined by others? Perhaps we did better in our initial belief, that the shivering cold is jointly experienced, something shared. I wonder. (6)

Other contemporary works articulate comparable notions. The narrator of Margaret Drabble's *The Waterfall* begins her story in the third person, but after fifty pages switches to the first person in the hopes of producing a more satisfactory narrative; in subsequent chapters, she alternates between the two perspectives. In Michel Tournier's *Friday* (1967), as Arlette Bouloumié has pointed out, a past tense, third person account alternates with a first person logbook, reflecting the thematic conflict between the man Crusoe was and the person he is becoming, as one form contaminates the other and results in "a triumph of the logbook and a victory for interiority" (Bouloumié, 454). Many examples of texts that shift between first and third person perspectives can be adduced, including Doris Lessing's *The Golden Notebook* (1962) and Marge Piercy's *He, She and It* (1991). Marguerite Duras's switching between the first and third person pronouns in *L'Amant* (1984) suggests a more self-reflexive and unsettling narrative topography. As Sharon Willis explains, "given the text's strategy of veiling and unveiling, where 'I' veils herself as 'she,' but where 'she' just as frequently masquerades as 'I,' we cannot maintain a rigid and secure separation of self and other, interior and exterior. Nor can we as readers determine a fixed vantage point, and the reassuring distance that would entail" (6).

In Roland Barthes's book, *Roland Barthes* (1975), we also find an oscillation between "I" and "he" segments, but one that also includes leading comments concerning the use of pronouns and the nature of writing one's life. ("All this must be considered as if spoken by a character in a novel—or rather by several characters," 119); "The intrusion, into the discourse of the essay, of a third person who nonetheless refers to no fictive creature, marks the necessity of remodeling the genres: let the essay show itself to be *almost* a novel: a novel without proper names" (120). By writing autobiographical fragments with techniques borrowed from contemporary fiction, Barthes not only problematizes the notion of genre, but also produces a Borgesian frame that keeps turning on itself. Andrew Brown observes that "[s]omebody in *Barthes par lui-meme* is saying *il,* framing Barthes: that somebody is a fictional character . . . but the *il* is not a *créature fictive:* Barthes has thus ensured that in such passages he has written a fiction whose (unnamed and unreal) soliloquist does nothing but discuss the (real) *il*" (124).

Christa Wolf, whose *Nachdenken über Christa T.* (1970) deftly mingled first and third person accounts, alternates between second and third person passages in *Kindheitsmuster* (1976), as the "I" is avoided and displaced by a "you" ("du"). As the narrator explains: "Allmählich, über Monate hin, stellte sich das Dilemma heraus: sprachlos bleiben oder in der dritten Person leben, das scheint zur Wahl zu stehen. Das eine unmöglich, unheimlich das andere" (9). ("Gradually, as months went by, the dilemma crystalized: to remain speechless, or else to live in the third person. The first is impossible, the second strange." [3]) At this point, the "unheimlich" second person narration commences. Throughout the novel, the second person is presented as more authentic, more responsible, and perhaps less subjective than the first person, though less arduous than the third. Assia Djebar's *A Sister to Scheherazade* shifts between first and second person perspectives; Carlos Fuentes's *Cambio de piel* (1967) and his recent *Inez* (2000) alternate between second and third person narration.

Anterior to nearly all of the examples I have adduced is Philippe Sollers's novel *Drame* (1965), which moves between a third person narrative of a writer and segments from that writer's first person fiction. Barthes has praised this text effusively: not only does it abolish the seemingly inevitable temporal distance between the experiencing self and the writing "I" who chronicles those events long after they occurred; it also refuses the distinction between first and third person positions: "Sollers alternates these two modes by a formal plan (the *he* and the *I* follow each other like the black and white squares on the chessboard) whose very rhetoric proclaims a purposely arbitrary quality" (in Sollers 91). The significance of this practice is worth some additional discussion.

Stanzel has written compellingly on the differences between first and third person narration and provided examples of authors who rewrote works from different narrative perspectives: Gottfried Keller's *Der Grüne Heinrich* (1912) was transposed from the third to the first person "with some hesitation and despite many misgivings" (83–84), while Kafka changed the first chapters of *Der Schloss* from the first to the third person. After discussing Henry James' quandary concerning how to present Strether's consciousness in *The Ambassadors*, Stanzel concludes, "many other authors besides James have racked their brains regarding the choice between the first- and third-person form, or else they have declared themselves emphatically for or against the former" (84). By depicting the same personage in both first and third person forms, Sollers underscores the artifice inherent in all fictional narration. Instead of choosing between one perspective or the other, or employing devices like inserted diaries or letters to provide a first person text within a third person narrative that does not violate any mimetic conventions, or even by having a first person narrator finally claim the third person materials, Sollers refuses to choose and thereby shows how fragile and perhaps arbitrary is the "foundational" distinction which differentiates, in Stanzel's words, "the identity and non-identity of the realms of existence of the fictional characters" (84). It is this conflation, which cannot normally be done in nonfictional or natural narratives, that is so unusual and so potentially disorienting, as is evident in the work of later authors who use multiple pronouns to refer to the same characters, such as Duras, Barthes, and, as we will see, Fuentes, McGahern, and Farah.

Together, these texts reveal distinctive characteristics of multiperson narrative: they present fresh possibilities for formal literary innovation and they create new methods to reinscribe thematic material at the level of narration, as the text's central concerns are embodied in a correlative formal technique. They can help a writer reproduce more accurately the jagged fissures within a single subjectivity; they can also provide alternative tools to define more sharply or collapse more effectively conventional distinctions between different characters, competing narrative worlds, or tale and frame. Thus, they can cunningly embody contemporary issues in philosophy, cultural studies, and gender theory relating to the reconfiguration of self, mind, and person. Perhaps most importantly, they allow the free play of multiple voices and can be seen as a practice that generates a greater degree of dialogism than more conventional techniques typically allow. This is no doubt why so many writers from previously marginalized or silenced groups have vigorously taken up multiperson narration. Gayle Greene notes it was astonishing that so many of the powerful feminist novels published in 1969 "implement the same device at the same time, using divided pronouns to express the sense of dividedness and contradiction. . . . Atwood and Drabble split their narratives into 'I' and 'she'; so too does [Patricia] Laurence, but she splits the narrative up into a veritable polyphony (or cacophony) of voices" (54–55).[3] I strongly suspect that this occurred primarily to give a more full and original expression to previously unnarratable thoughts and perspectives, even though we may suggest that there is nothing inherently female or feminist about writing in the first person, as will be discussed at greater length toward the end of this chapter.

Many of the distinctive features of multiperson novels figure even more prominently in the small group of unusually resonant fictions that juxtapose first, second, and third person narration. Juan Goytisolo's *Paisajes después de la batalla* (1982) ingeniously manipulates reader identification and response through a deviously compelling play with narrative person. The shifting use of the narrative "you" is used to establish an identity between the reader and the dispossessed peoples living in and around Paris, as well as with a xenophobic racist and child molester. More systematic interrogations of the three major narrational pronouns appear in Carlos Fuentes' *The Death of Artemio Cruz* (1962), John McGahern's *The Dark* (1969), and Nuruddin Farah's *Maps* (1986). Fuentes' novel explores the transformation of its complex protagonist from idealistic revolutionary to oppressive oligarch and, by extension, chronicles the concomitant degeneration of the Mexican revolution. The book is presented in a series of triadic alternations, as a first person present tense section is followed by a third person past tense segment which in turn is succeeded by a second person passage written (sometimes rather affectedly) in the future tense. All three modes of narration center on the protagonist; the third person passages however occasionally stray and present thoughts and events unknown to him—most poignantly, the last thoughts of his son before his own untimely death in Spain. The first person sections, following modernist, post-Joycean conventions, adhere quite closely to the successive thoughts of Cruz in his final hours. The second person segments are rather more dynamic: they fragment and coalesce, range over different time periods, and include quasi- or nonnarrative material. The final two segments fuse the different narrating voices as the protagonist expires: "Yo no sé . . . no sé . . . si él soy yo . . . si tú fue el . . . si yo soy los tres . . . Tú . . . te traigo dentro de mí y vas a morir conmigo" (1974: 1407) ("I don't know . . . don't know . . . I am he or if . . . you were he . . . or if I am the three . . . You . . . I carry you inside me and you will die with me . . . [1964: 305]); this passage is directly followed by the final second person text which likewise ends in a fusion of perspectives that is equated with death: "'Artemio Cruz . . . Nombre . . . "inútil" . . . "corazón" . . . "masaje" . . . "inútil" . . . ya no sabrás . . . te traje adentro y moriré contigo . . . los tres . . . moriremos . . . Tú . . . mueres . . . has muerto . . . moriré" (1974: 1408). ("Artemio Cruz . . . Name . . . Hopeless . . . heart massage . . . hopeless . . . You will not know now. I carry you inside and with you I die. The three, we . . . will die. You . . . die, have died . . . I will die" [1964: 306]). There is a final collapsing, or perhaps more precisely, evacuating, of the three narrating positions and the three tenses. A closure is attained, both for the protagonist and for the text's drama of experimental techniques; significantly, it is one that refuses to reduce any one voice to either of the others.

McGahern's *The Dark* begins with four chapters of third person narration, moves on to a chapter in the first person, and then presents several chapters in the second person, all of which depict the same individual. The ending of the book largely follows the opposite trajectory, as some pages in the first person are followed by four chapters in the third, though in the final pages the "you" reasserts itself. Though it is difficult to identify a clear thematic pattern that governs these pronominal shifts, it appears that "you" narration predominates when the protagonist is establishing his own subjectivity against the voices, names, and desires that others seek to impose on him: "If you stood and stopped the crazy fighting within yourself you'd be able to see what the noise inside the gates was" (176). In the third person segments his social identity is relatively stable, while in the first person passages he tends to be fixated on his temporarily stable self.

In Farah's *Maps,* as Rhonda Cobham points out, the shifting uncertainties of nation, sexuality, and history are mirrored in the text's "use of three personal pronouns to narrate Askar's story. Askar identifies these at the end of the novel as the voices of judge, witness, and audience (246), although, typically, the lines between these three perspectives are not always reliably indicated by the pronoun used" (49). Each narrative voice both obscures and reveals different information, and does so in an idiosyncratic tone. The first person narrative is rather diffident and at times almost willfully ignorant of the surrounding circumstances; the second person narration is on the other hand vague, oneiric, and suspiciously vatic. The third person narration, though not without its own archetypal ambiance, is more objective, limiting, and distant. It is precisely these differences that foreground the paramount significance of the category of person for narrative theory and analysis.

Genette, as we have noted, affirms: "The novelist's choice, unlike the narrator's, is not between two grammatical forms, but between two narrative postures (whose grammatical forms are simply an automatic consequence): to have the story told by one of its 'characters,' or to have it told by a narrator outside of the story" (244). But this is exactly what Fuentes, McGahern, and Farah refuse to do, and much of the power of these works results precisely from a rejection of the dichotomous position within which Genette would attempt to circumscribe these texts. Instead of choosing between two narrative positions, these authors elect to employ three. Another ambiguity attends the novels' three-person narrative form. Unlike *Bleak House,* in which Esther Summerson's first person account can be neatly placed within a larger, extra- and heterodiegetic whole, the three narrations of *Artemio Cruz* refuse to fall into any epistemological hierarchy. We cannot determine whether Cruz is telling his story using three different pronouns, or an extra- and heterodiegetic narrator is employing all three forms, or whether two or three distinct narrators are at work. The same is the case (though somewhat less spectacularly) for the other triple-voiced narrations. It is precisely this irreducible ambiguity that gives the novel its peculiar tension and urges theorists to extend our analytical categories.

This conclusion is perhaps even more evident when one considers Maurice Roche's *Compact* (1966), probably the *ne plus ultra* of multiperson narrative. Its multiple, symmetrical, and curiously parallel story lines are narrated in a nearly exhaustive range of possible pronouns that foreground the insistence and complexity of the category of narrative person. The reader is presented with you (*tu*), one (*on*), I, he, we, and even a passive voice narration devoid of pronominal reference.

The power of the alternating narrations is often most evident in transitions from one form to another:

> J'avais beau ma direque claquer était à la portée de tout le monde, que ce serait une bonne chose de faite, le coeur n'y était pas.
>
> "— . . . *humble medecin est une hypnotiseur parfait; au besoin, il utise protoxide d'azote . . . operation benigne . . .*" IL S'AGISSAIT DE LUI ÉPARGNER TOUTE SOUFFRANCE.
>
> **Tu ne sentiras rien. Tout se passera à ton insu; tu pourrais aussi bien ne pas être là; mais loin, hors de tout.** (70)

> I could tell myself a million times that turning it was within everyone's reach, that it would be a deed well done, my heart just wasn't in it.
>
> "— . . . *humble doctor is perfect hypnotist; if necessary, he uses nitrous oxide . . . benign operation . . .*" IT WAS A MATTER OF SPARING HER PAIN.
>
> **You'll feel nothing. Everything will happen without your knowing it. You could just as well not be there, but far away, outside of everything.** (58)

The meticulous, contrapuntal braiding of distinct voices (and the independent stories they narrate) in this text clearly indicates person to be an indispensable category of narrative analysis. The fact that, as many critics have observed, some of the different narrative voices seem to merge together testifies to the need for particular suppleness within such an analytical perspective.[4]

Looking back over the range of examples set forth above, we may discern two major tendencies: a centrifugal one, which produces ever more possibilities of narration, and juxtaposes storytelling from first person, third person, and still other perspectives, as additional viewpoints and positionalities are included in the act of narration. These may be presented by the inclusion of more voices and more kinds of voice, or they may take the form of more perspectives that narrate the world of a single figure, as we see quite prominently in Fuentes' *Artemio Cruz*. The other tendency is a centripetal one, in which genuinely or apparently distinct voices are either contained within a single mind or collapsed into another voice. The first of these is represented by the alternating "he" and "you" sections of Beckett's *Company* that turn out to be merely different registers of the same voice; the second by the multiplicity of different acts of narration impossibly run together in *The Unnamable*. These examples in turn suggest a final possibility—the suggestion of multiple voices that nevertheless cannot be identified with precision but which remain ambiguous, shuttling between one mind and many, as demonstrated so compellingly by Nathalie Sarraute's texts. In every case we see a move away from the simple, unproblematic categories of first and third person narration. The collective richness of these works and their challenging effects on readers demonstrate convincingly the importance of person as a category of narrative theory and analysis even as they show that the concept of person must be substantially expanded to include second person, multiperson, and "impossible" narration.

In the history of narrative theory we can find an intriguing precedent for the position I am advocating. In 1927, E. M. Forster attacked the univocal categories propounded by Percy Lubbock and praised instead *Bleak House* and Gide's *Les Faux monnayeurs,* works in which omniscient narration, limited omniscience, and first person forms alternate. Forster concluded:

> A novelist can shift his viewpoint if it comes off, and it came off with Dickens and Tolstoy. Indeed this power to expand and contract perception (of which the shifting view-point is a symptom), this right to intermittent knowledge:—I find it one of the great advantages of the novel-form, and it has a parallel in our perception of life. We are stupider at some times than others; we can enter into people's minds occasionally but not always. (81)

It is unfortunate that this thesis of Forster's has been critically overlooked for so long by Lubbock's varied followers and successors in narratology.

The second point Forster makes in this passage—the relation between the strategies of narration and lived social experience—has drawn a great deal more attention, particularly in the numerous quests to not merely identify general ideological tendencies but equate one form of narration with a specific political agenda. For almost a century theorists have debated the ideological valence of the choice of person in narration. Glancing back over some of these controversies, one is struck by the vehemence of the argumentation, the abrupt shifts in position over what is "revolutionary" and what "reactionary" from decade to decade, and the general ephemerality of moments of consensus. We may begin by noting Georg Lukacs' influential strictures against modernist subjectivism that provided the most powerful theoretical justification for decades of socialist realism. In the 1940s, the

Sartre-Mauriac dispute recast the debate as Sartre denounced third person omniscient narration as inherently inauthentic. Roland Barthes is perhaps the most persuasive of recent ideological apologists for first person narration. In *Writing Degree Zero,* he observed that third person narration "attracts the most conformist and the least dissatisfied" (35); two decades later, as noted in my introductory chapter, Barthes would go on to state that "'he' is wicked: the nastiest word in the language: pronoun of the non-person, it annuls and mortifies its referent; . . . Saying 'he' about someone, I always envision a kind of murder by language . . ." (169). Though more sophisticated and paradoxical than his earlier simple denunciation of third person narration, Barthes' aversion to the third person is clear, and echoes comparable statements by Robbe-Grillet and others.[5] Recently, some new historicists have denounced third person narration as an analogue of the panopticon and related methods of surveillance and control.[6]

While we may sympathize with the general position behind these remarks—that third person omniscient narration tends to reify and "naturalize" existing social relations—the fact remains that, among writers who alternate from book to book between first and third person narratives (Dickens, Thackeray, Conrad, Calvino, Wittig), we don't usually find the first person narratives more emancipatory than the others; sometimes, indeed, we don't immediately remember whether a given text is narrated in one person or the other. Furthermore, many works of certain avowed fascists and fascist sympathizers (Hamsun, Céline, Cela) employ a particularly intense kind of first person narration. These examples would seem to definitively refute any claims for the liberatory nature of first person narration. In the last chapter we saw how radically opposed positions have similarly employed "we" narration; elsewhere I have outlined the radically different ideological valences that have been associated with second person narration ("Linearity" 689–90). It is clear that no form has any inherent essence or tendency—or at least none that a competent practitioner cannot readily circumvent. Ideological stances are frequently associated with practices of narration, but to affirm that there is a simple progressive or conservative "essence" to any particular technique is certainly erroneous.

Feminist attempts to move beyond sexist cultural binaries have not produced a consistent position concerning narration. Joanne S. Frye, in a chapter on "the subversive I," articulates what was then a common position. She writes that for female writers, to "speak directly in a personal voice is to deny the exclusive right of male author-ity implicit in a public voice and to escape the expression of dominant ideologies upon which an omniscient narrator depends" (51). She goes on to explain:

> If a female pronoun recurs throughout a text it repeatedly reminds us of cultural expectations for what it means to be female; it reminds us, inevitably, of the [patriarchy's] femininity text. The "I," by contrast, reminds us only of a subjective narrating presence, a nameless agent; it asks us to remember only its subjective agency. The "she" can easily lull us into conventional expectations; the "I" keeps us conscious of possibility and change. (65)

This value-laden binary opposition, at once suggestive and familiar, necessarily invites scrutiny of the terms it rests upon. First of all it tends to replicate rather than contest what Susan S. Lanser, in her discussion of *Bleak House* cited earlier, identified as "the ideology of separate spheres" (*Fictions* 240), a division many feminists might well be reluctant to see codified so decisively. In addition, many might question the subversive or liberating value posited in the first person pronoun. Virginia Woolf, it will be remembered, quickly became bored by a representative male writer's insistent use of the first person: "After reading a chapter or two a shadow seemed to lie across the page. It was a dark, straight bar, a shadow shaped something like the letter 'I.' One began dodging this way and that to catch a glimpse of the landscape behind it. Whether that was indeed a tree or a woman walking I was not quite sure. Back one was always hailed to the letter 'I'. One began to be tired of 'I'" (103). Far from erasing or eluding gender markers, the "I" of the male writer is utterly self-absorbed and altogether too self-sufficient. Adelaide Morris shows how women writers gradually moved away from a suspicion of the many negative implications of this pronoun documented by Woolf and others earlier in the twentieth century before embracing it—often in a highly qualified manner—in the sixties (11–17). Trinh T. Minh-ha offers a different perspective, suggesting that the pronoun "I," far from being monolithic, is in fact multivalent: it includes not only "I (the all-knowing subject)" but "I/i (the plural, non-unitary subject)" and "i (the personal race- and gender-specific subject)" (9–11). Once again, we may look to the work of Elizabeth Jane Howard to help us verify or dismiss some of these claims. In her recent novel, *Falling* (1999), she reveals how the now conventionally gendered dyad of "I" and "he" can be effortlessly inverted. This text alternates between the first person writing of a predatory male and the third person account that is focalized solely through the unsuspecting female protagonist.[7]

The feminist quest for a discursive site beyond the first person is perhaps most emphatically articulated by Monique Wittig in the author's note that prefaces *Le corps lesbien* (1975). She states that the "je," when written by a woman, is always alienating since that "I" must write in a language that denies and negates female experience. Every such usage is always already reinscribed within a larger masculine matrix (10). All of the limitations Frye attributes to the use of "she" are present for Wittig in the writing of "*je.*" Consequently, Wittig says she is physically incapable of writing "*je*"; instead, her novel is narrated by a "*j/e,*" an ideologically marked pronoun that desires "to do violence by writing to the language which *I* [*j/e*] can enter only by force" (10).[8] Similarly, Frye's position seems to be controverted by Maxine Hong Kingston's observation: "There is a Chinese word for the female *I*—which is 'slave.'" Kingston affirms that such a usage attempts to break "the women with their own tongues" (47).

In her essay "The Three *Genres,*" Luce Irigaray makes an important observation in her analysis of male and female pronominal usage, the first part of which might serve as a gloss on Woolf's remarks: "With men, the *I* is asserted in different ways; it is significantly more important than the *you* and *the world.* With women, the *I* often makes way for the *you, the world,* for the objectivity of words and things" (146). Women's discourse, even in the first person, often remains other-directed, seeking interaction and validation. Men, on the other hand, "live within the closed universe of the first-person pronoun; their messages are often self-affirmations which leave little space for co-creation with an *other* sex," writes Margaret Whitford, summarizing Irigaray's position (Irigaray, 78). This postulate can help explain why a number of feminist writers have moved beyond the "I" to the more fluid, interactive, and destabilizing technique of "we" narration, as noted in the last chapter, and second person narration as found in works like those of Mary McCarthy, Edna O'Brien, Lorrie Moore, and Jamaica Kincaid, as well as other texts like Pam Houston's "How to Talk to a Hunter" and Sunetra Gupta's *The Glassblower's Breath.* It is also suggests specific ideological reasons for other feminists' deployments of still other pronouns —most strikingly, *on* and *elles* in Wittig's *L'Opoponax* (1964) and *Les Guerilleres* (1969)— and for the alternation and/or conflation of the first, second, and third person pronouns in previously mentioned works by Lispector, Sontag, Wolf, Weldon, and Duras. One may, in conclusion, applaud the efforts of feminist writers (and, by extension, those of colonized subjects and sexual and ethnic minorities) to contest undeniable social prejudices inherent in existing linguistic practice, even as one acknowledges that no mode of narration has any inherent ideological valence.[9]

There is one final, distinctively postmodern category of multiple narration to identify, and that is the category of "impossible narration": metaleptic texts that contain discourse that cannot possibly be spoken or written by their purported narrators and may involve the kind of ontological framebreaking typical of postmodern works. A paradigmatic example of this kind of text is Christine Brooke-Rose's *Thru* (1975), which is succinctly described by Shlomith Rimmon-Kenan in the following terms: "The novel repeatedly reverses the hierarchy [of narrative levels], transforming a narrated object into a narrating agent and vice versa. The very distinction between outside and inside, container and contained, narrating subject and narrated object, higher and lower level collapses, resulting in a paradox which the text itself puts in a nutshell: 'Whoever you invented invented you too.'" (94).

This practice, which can only occur in works of fiction, may extend as far back as Diderot's *Jacques le fataliste* and is not uncommon in recent French fiction, notably Beckett's *The Unnamable* and the later novels of Robbe-Grillet. *The Unnamable,* as we will see, simultaneously enacts several of the different extreme possibilities of narration. The narrative voice often refers to other characters and voices which it then discloses to be fictions invented by itself, as apparently independent persons are collapsed into a single narrative voice. On the other hand, the same narrator goes on to claim to have invented the frustrated narrators of other novels written by Beckett; the narrator of *The Unnamable* here seems to be impersonating its author. This narrative strategy does not merely problematize conventional theoretical distinctions, but undermines the very terms upon which such distinctions rest.

Once again, we see how traditional narrative theory, implicitly based on the more stable nonfictional types of biography (third person) and autobiography (first person), have a difficult time comprehending forms that, like second person and impossible narration, do not or cannot occur in nonfictional discourse. Up to now, narrative theory has tended to deny, ignore, or dismiss as inconsequential curiosities the

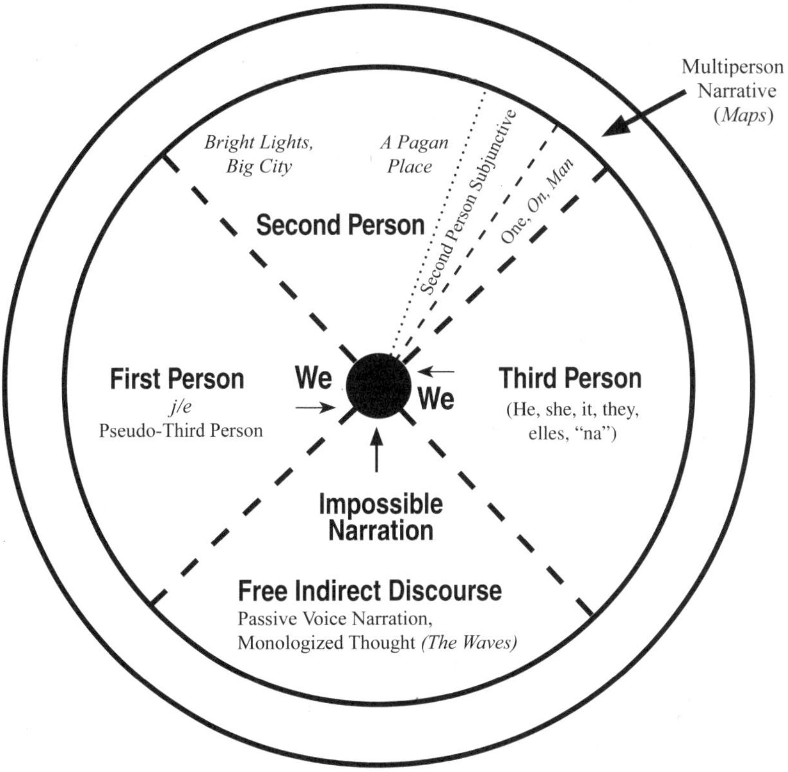

Figure 1. Strategies of Narration.

very kinds of narration that are distinctively fictional. The fundamental question is, once again, Which model of narrative is more effective for theorizing the practice of fiction: one grounded in linguistics and imitations of nonfictional narratives, or one that begins with the heterogeneity, polymorphism, and flagrant fictionality typical of the novel from Petronius and Lucian to Beckett and Wittig?

If, as I have argued, the latter is the case, it is necessary to remap strategies of narration in a more expansive and dialectical manner. Recalling Stanzel's "narrative circle," which uses a subtly gradated illustration of narrative person, we can now envisage an alternative model that is more comprehensive and flexible. I would like to argue for a four-part division of such a circle as shown in figure 1. The quadrant on the left would cover first person narration; its opposite, on the right, would include third person forms. At the bottom, connecting the two, free indirect discourse can be situated; at the top, the long neglected category of second person narration can take its rightful place. Second person novels that incline toward other forms of presentation may be situated accordingly: Jay McInerney's *Bright Lights, Big City* would be near the first person boundary, while Edna O'Brien's *A Pagan Place* should reside near the space of the third person.

We may further subdivide this circle to include a number of recent innovative deployments of person. Nonmimetic "we" narratives stretch synthetically from the first to the third person. "One" narration (*on, man*), which can approximate much of the same conceptual space as "you" forms, rests uncomfortably between second and third person forms, adjacent to the "hypothetical" second person mode, in which a narratee/protagonist is given instructions that form a narrative.[10] Moving on to the third person, we observe how this category can be extended to include works that refer largely to a collective "they" (Perec's *Les Choses,* 1965), an "it," and "na," the gender-neutral pronoun invented by June Arnold for her novel, *The cook and the carpenter* (1973). It is in the bottom quadrant that we may most plausibly situate the sustained use of the passive voice that denies person and minimizes agency, as deployed in Kathy Acker's story "Humility," also present in Conrad's *Narcissus* and Roche's *Compact.* This agentless form will edge up against the boundary of free indirect discourse; in the same quadrant we may add the "monologized thought" employed by Woolf in *The Waves* to the standard category of free indirect discourse.

To conclude our mapping of narrational possibilities, it will be helpful to draw another circle around the first circle to represent the flow of multiperson narratives that travel across or beyond the ordinary divisions and juxtapose divergent points of view. Lastly, I would like to propose that a large black dot occupy the center of the figure, to stand for impossible and impossibly conflated acts of narration. Only with such a Borgesian schema can one embrace the kinds of functions produced by authors like, well, Borges.

Three Extreme Forms of Narration and a Note on Postmodern Unreliability

chapter five

In this chapter I will explore three of the most significant and extreme narrating agents which exist at the very boundaries of narration: 1) the figure of the interlocutor, or disembodied questioning voice, as it appears in *Ulysses* and in recent fiction, 2) denarration, in which a narrator negates or erases aspects of the world created by the narration, and 3) what I call the "permeable narrator," a speaker who says "I" but whose narration transgresses the natural limits of the contents and perceptions of a single consciousness. I will then go on to identify a number of distinctively postmodern types of unreliable narrator.

I. The Interlocutor

The interlocutor is a disembodied voice that poses questions which the narrative goes on to answer. It should be differentiated from superficially similar textual phenomena in order to specify what this figure (or function) is not. It is, after all, rather common to encounter a voice within the diegesis of a fictional text that poses questions. Most of the time, it is relatively easy to identify the speaker and to describe the speech situation it enacts; it usually takes one of three forms. Take the lines, "You were a student weren't you? Of what in the other devil's name? Paysayenn. P.C.N., you know: *physiques, chimiques, et naturelles.*

Aha." (*U* 3.175–77). In this bit of free indirect discourse from the Proteus episode of *Ulysses,* Stephen Dedalus is talking to himself, carrying on in his own mind a remembered or imagined dialogue with another.

For a second example, we may go to the narrator of Dickens' *Bleak House,* who asks the following partially rhetorical question to his narratee at the beginning of the sixteenth chapter: "What connexion can there be, between the place in Lincolnshire, the house in town, the Mercury in powder, and the whereabout of Jo the outlaw . . . ?" We readily recognize this as a common feature of eighteenth and nineteenth century fiction, as the narrator articulates likely or suitable questions that either the narrative or authorial audience might have. Indeed, Sterne frequently parodied such colloquies. Up to this point, there is no problem at all in identifying and situating the various questioners or questioning voices in these texts.[1] Issues of person, narration, and audience are clear; there is no need to look beyond Stanzel, Genette, Chatman, or Prince.

But even fairly standard examples can easily become deviant. Near the beginning of *Notes from the Underground,* for example, we meet with the following lines: "Advantage! What is advantage? Can you possibly give an exact definition of advantage? . . . What do you think? Are there cases where it is so? You are laughing?" (279). Dostoevsky's narrator is envisioning responses with such precision that they may point to an origin in the narrator's obsessions rather than any mimesis of others' probable speech. In *The Good Soldier,* Ford Madox Ford's narrator Dowell playfully personifies his narratee (who here may be indiscernible from Ford's authorial audience): "Is all this a digression or isn't it digression? Again I don't know. You, the listener, sit opposite me. But you are so silent. You don't tell me anything" (19). Here, the narratee is playfully chided for the silence that this particular narrative contract enjoins him to maintain. We will see, however, that the category confusion implicit in Dowell's remarks nicely presages some of the conflations and ambiguous relations between teller and hearer that would soon appear in the history of narrative.

A number of recent works of fiction employ an unidentified, unmarked narrative voice that asks questions that the narrative proper then responds to; for much or all of the text it is not clear what the status of these voices are; whether they emanate from a single source or whether they are irreducibly dual. The ease with which a new questioning voice can materialize is evident in Diderot's short text entitled, "This is not a Story" (ca. 1772). The work begins with the narrator noting that, since in an oral storytelling situation there is invariably a listener who interrupts the tale to ask questions, he has introduced an inquisitive character "whose role is more or less that of the reader" (45). This character narratee would seem to have made good use of his new body, since a few pages into the text he admits to having had an affair with the woman the narrator is infatuated with. Thus, a textual function can readily become a character proper; the opposite movement is also possible, as we will see in the case of Beckett's projected pseudo-characters.

The source of most modern experiments is the "Ithaca" episode of Joyce's *Ulysses,* and it is with this text that we may most appropriately begin our analysis. The chapter consists of some 2300 lines of questions and answers. Joyce identifies the episode's technique as "catechism, impersonal," a designation that makes specifying the exact nature of this elusive text still more daunting. At one level, it suggests earlier critiques of compulsory catechistic instruction made by Blake and Byron; at another level, it is itself a very strange kind of anti-catechism, couched in exaggerated scientistic language and containing much more narrative and description than standard doctrine or useful knowledge.

Furthermore, the catechism itself is a somewhat unusual discursive practice; as Robert Hampson points out, it "has the form of a dialogue, [though] it is monologic: the questions and answers constitute a repertoire which the respondent is required to learn. The respondent does not respond personally to the question but rather internalises the answer which the questioner has already supplied" (230).[2] The catechism is thus a text with a single implied author and single voice or perspective to be performed by more than one individual. Joyce of course immediately strays from this orthodox arrangement, and goes on to test the limits of the question and answer format. In doing so, however, he retains and intensifies the catechism's inversion of the function of dialogue and problematizes further the status of the speaking subject. We may legitimately wonder just who the speaker is (or who the speakers are) of the following exchange that begins the episode:

> What parallel courses did Bloom and Stephen follow returning?
>
> Starting united both at normal walking pace from Beresford place they followed in the order named Lower and Middle Gardiner streets and Mountjoy Square, west: then, at reduced pace, each bearing left, Gardiner's place by an inadvertence as far as the farther corner of

> Temple street: then, at reduced pace with interruptions of halt, bearing right, Temple street, north, as far as Hardwicke place. . . . (*U* 17.1–7)

This passage, which is fairly representative of most in the rest of the chapter, is rife with ambiguities concerning its nature, status, and speech situation. Is this a catechism proper or a series of genuine questions and answers? Are we to understand this text as written or spoken? Is there one speaker or two? That is, is the questioner an independent character, a stylistic feature that serves as a pretext for the dissemination of the material that follows the question, or could it be a personification of the narratee? David Hayman has rather famously (at least in Joycean circles) posited the figure of what he calls "the arranger" to designate the sensibility responsible for the many different voices and effects beyond those of *Ulysses*'s primary narrator, who "practically disappears" after "Sirens" (91). Is this, then, the arranger?

One might also ask other questions, such as what is the possible speech situation of such pointlessly precise information in the episode? Or perhaps the entire chapter is best read as a kind of allegory of mis- or noncommunication. In the passages that follow the one I have cited, we do not get anything resembling definitive answers to these questions; instead, the multiple ambiguities increase. Fritz Senn argues that the question and answer format is itself merely a kind of stylistic pretext: "'Ithaca' aspires toward successive enumeration, silent as in writing, in spite of the presence of a questioning and answering voice. Such voices are disembodied conveniences, with no ostensible attribution. The dual form is a communicative stratagem" (38).[3]

The typologically resistant nature of Joyce's text can be brought into relief by comparing it with Pinget's novel, *The Inquisitory,* which superficially seems quite similar in the use of this technique. Here too an interrogative is asked in a single line of type, "Yes or no answer," without any quotation markers or punctuation, and it is responded to in equally unmarked lines. The response, however, rapidly provides substantial information about the man being questioned. We quickly learn that he is a servant in a large house, that he had lived and worked there for several years, that he is speaking directly to the interlocutor, and so forth. None of this information is available to the reader of *Ulysses.*

A key feature of these figures, both in "Ithaca" and in many subsequent texts that employ an interlocutor, is the protean nature of both questioner and respondent. In *Ulysses,* the primary function of the interlocutor seems to alternate between producing repetitions of prearranged answers and providing queries that seek out new information, as in the following: "Did either openly allude to their racial difference? / Neither" (17.525–26), or when the interlocutor requests amplification of an earlier statement ("Such as?" 17.587; "What?" 17.618; "Then?" 17.2240). At other points a genuine though brief dialogue appears to be in the process of emerging, as the respondent provides the information desired by the interlocutor when a more strict answer would prove misleading ("Was this affirmation apprehended by Bloom?/ Not verbally. Substantively" (17.1017–18). These transformations conclude with the interlocutor's call for clarification, "Womb? Weary?" (17.2319) and the respondent's stumbling attempts to answer the text's final three questions, With? When? and Where?[4] The second of these take him beyond the edge of identity, logic, and meaning: "Going to dark bed there was a square round Sinbad the Sailor roc's auk's egg in the night of the bed of all the auks of the rocs of Darkinbad the Brightdayler" (17.2328–30). The last question, "Where?" leads the respondent beyond speech (and, for that matter, the conventions of typography) as the response is indicated merely by a large dot: • .

Such transformations in the nature and status of the interlocutor in subsequent fiction are common, indeed fairly standard. Pinget's respondent, referred to above, also undergoes a substantial metamorphosis, and the text itself turns into a parable of the act of writing fiction: "I'm not here any more we could invent other people no matter who yes make them say anything we liked it would be just like what happened to the real ones all of them in our heads they're dead, your questions give me the impression we're forcing them to speak but mistakes are not important they'd talk just the same whether it's true or false" (247–48). At the end of Beckett's *Molloy,* a series of questions of a theological nature are set forth in the style of a catechism, though no answers emerge. In many of his later works, the main epistemological drama of the text is often the determination of the identity of the speaker and hearer of an endless stream of questions or demands. This is especially true of *The Unnamable,* as we will see in the third section of this chapter. One quotation will suffice us here: "But who is he, if my guess is right, who is waiting for that, from me? And who these others whose designs are so different? And into whose hands I play when I ask myself such questions? But do I, do I? In the jar did I ask myself questions?" (331). Beckett here employs a cascade of questions but entirely obscures their discursive status by making it unclear how serious they are, which person is being spoken of, and even whether they have an addressee other than the speaker himself. He later self-consciously refers to the catechistic method in the text but, significantly, renders its status paradoxical: "They have no pedagogic purpose in view, that's definite. There is no question of imparting to him any instruction whatsoever, for the moment. This catechist's tongue, honeyed and perfidious, is the only one they know" (356). The identity of the "they" is irreducibly ambiguous.

More extreme are the unmotivated questions that irrupt into the body of the text in Robbe-Grillet's novels *La Maison de rendez-vous* and *Project for a Revolution in New York*. Some of these include hostile objections to the narrative as a whole: "Don't you have a tendency to insist too much, as I have already indicated, on the erotic aspects of the scenes you report?" (*Project* 159). Bruce Morrisette describes a set of these in *Project* in the following terms: "At this point in the text occurs a new type of interrogatory sequence, in which the narrator replies to objections made by someone who seems to combine the (analogous?) qualities of chief of an organization and literary critic. The narrator defends the eroticism of his descriptions, his exaggerations, the unidiomatic distortions of some New York place names, and even the use of the term 'cut' to punctuate his text (despite the fact that 'cut' will so appear only later)" (*Novels* 277). These introjections are rather extreme cases of the kinds of disruptions the interlocutor frequently or even typically occasions. As such, they strike me as being situated at varying distances between the roles of the narrator and the narratee, though difficult to reduce to either.

Joyce Carol Oates uses an interlocutor that slides between the hetero- and homodiegetic levels in her story, "What Is the Connection Between Men and Women?" (1970). A more extreme deployment of the interlocutor appears in Jeanette Winterson's short text, "The Poetics of Sex." Here, six rude rhetorical questions presented in a large font appear. They are answered indirectly and obliquely by a creative respondent who produces a highly metaphorical love narrative as a partial (or pretended) response. The interlocutor does not appear able to understand or even hear these answers, and the respondent does not seem to expect them to be heard. It is a parody of a dialogue, a total transformation of the question and answer scenario. Instead of eliciting information, the questions serve to generate the narrative. In this, it is typical of the way the postmodern interlocutor and respondent defy conventional norms, particularly (but not exclusively) the primordial one between narrator and (dramatized) narratee.

Winterson's story, however, differs from most of the other deployments in that the two voices are entirely self-consistent. A glance back at "Ithaca" readily discloses how radically different each voice grows. The respondent is particularly multiform as his speech includes, as we have seen, pointlessly pedestrian information, obsessively scientistic descriptions, some dubious lyricism—"The heaventree of stars hung with humid nightblue fruit" (1039)—and a repetitive eroticism that merges with the scientistic discourse and finally produces a curious lyricism: "He kissed the plump mellow yellow smellow melons of her rump, on each melonous hemisphere, in their mellow yellow furrow, with obscure prolonged provocative mellonsmellonous osculation" (2241–43).

Does a single subject or voice produce this heterogenous discourse? Karen Lawrence notes that although she uses "the term 'narrator' for ease of reference," she prefers "the concept of consciousness or mind of the text, since Joyce does everything possible in 'Ithaca' to destroy our sense of a narrating, human voice" (183–84). This strikes me as an eminently sound critical move; we have posthumanist narration without a single, self-consistent, identifiable narrator. Concerning *Ulysses* as a whole, Timothy Martin has observed that "the end of the novel is so different from the beginning that it might almost have been written by a different writer" (207); this refusal to remain confined within the boundaries of a single human voice also informs the discourse of several of the later chapters of the work, including "Ithaca." Just as two or more individuals may collaborate and form a single implied author, here a single historical author is constructing radically incommensurate voices that may not be reduced to a single postulated human psyche.

I wish to suggest that the interlocutor, as depicted above, is an unstable and inherently protean figure (or kind of discourse) that regularly oscillates from one function or status to another as it evokes familiar categories like narrator and narratee in order to blur their edges or transgress them altogether. As such it would seem to be a new category that deserves inclusion in a poetics that attempts to circumscribe the narrative experiments of *Ulysses* and postmodern fiction. In this, it resembles the phenomenon of second person narration, which often resembles yet eludes the adjacent forms of first and third person narration.

I will go on to suggest that even if one proposes, as many might first be inclined to do, that in most of the cases adduced so far we really only need a single, albeit highly flexible narrator, and that the notion of a personified narratee is, following the trajectory of certain texts of Beckett, merely the illusory projection of a single voice in a vain attempt to successfully create or ventriloquize another, still we will have to look hard at the curious nature of the single prolific narrator (or should we say supernarrator?) we have now evoked. In virtually all of these cases (some of them quite dramatically), the narrative discourse thus predicated of the single narrational source far exceeds the standard range or limits of any single human sensibility. Such a move would "solve" the question of the interlocutor only to replace it with the conundrum of a shapeless, contradictory, indeed monstrous supernarrator. In fact, any possible collocation of any heterogenous discourses could always be projected as the work of a single narrator bent on producing irreducible heterogeneity. This does not strike me as a satisfactory solution. Put another way, the author may create a narrator that is psychologically and historically consistent, or she may produce discourse that cannot be plausibly located within a single human speaker; it does not seem useful or accurate to refer to each discourse simply as the work of a narrator, since the latter case violates all the parameters that govern the former. That is, the concept of a narrator implies a certain minimal discursive consistency that many late modern and postmodern authors reject; we should have a place for shifting, depersonalized, multivoiced texts that transcend or traduce the sensibility of a single narrator, a composite figure we may refer to as the "incommensurate narrator."

Here we are running up once more against the implicit mimetic presuppositions of conventional notions of the narrator. As we noted at the beginning of this book, Wolfgang Kayser stated this quite explicitly: once we lose sight of the notion that the narrator is someone who tells a story, the novel is dead (*Entstehung*, 34). For many postmodern authors, however, the death of the traditional narrator is the essential precondition for the creation of new forms with other, disparate, decentered voices. We should not insist on a humanistic frame to encompass overt narration, even if it was produced by a single human being. Structuralist narratology has performed a great service by revealing that characters can be conceived both as humanlike entities and as textual functions. The same insight should be readily applied to narrators: on the one hand, they may well resemble actual people who tell stories; on the other hand, there may be no "they" there—with postmodern fiction, we often have mere discourse that unconvincingly occupies the space of a standard narrator. It is this rejection of the personified narrator that the figure of the interlocutor finally reveals.

II. Denarration

We may now move on to an intriguing and paradoxical strategy of narration that I will call "denarration." I am referring to a kind of narrative negation in which a narrator denies significant aspects of his or her narrative that had earlier been presented as given. The simplest example of this might be something like, "Yesterday it was raining. Yesterday it was not raining." The effect of this unusual strategy is variable: it can play a relatively minor role in the overall text, or it can fundamentally alter the nature and reception of the story. The effect it produces is nearly always arresting, and to many readers it can be quite disconcerting. In what follows, I will present several instances of this practice, analyze its functions within a text, and go on to speculate on its import for narrative theory.

For a sustained and relentless deployment of denarration, we may look to Samuel Beckett, a master of the art of verbal negation. Early on in *Molloy,* the narrator states that, while he was sitting on a rock, he saw characters A and C walking slowly towards each other. This transpired on a road remarkably bare, "I mean without hedges or ditches"; the narrator is sure this took place in the country, since "cows were chewing in enormous fields" (8). He admits that he is perhaps "inventing a little, perhaps embellishing"; nevertheless, we are assured that "on the whole that's the way it was" (8). The addition of this qualification serves to enhance one's sense of the narrator's reliability. This simple narration of an ordinary event is, however, quickly called into question by another statement a little further into the text: "And I am perhaps confusing several different occasions, and different times, deep down. . . . And perhaps it was A at one day at one place, then C another at another, then a third the rock and I, and so on for the other components, the cows, the sky, the sea, the mountains" (17). Now, the causal and temporal relations are rendered dubious; all that remains are the elements themselves, devoid of their relation to one another. They can, it would seem, be recombined in any number of different constellations. Of course, if the causal and temporal relations are so easily negated, the solidity of the other figures becomes considerably less firm. Is it certain that there was, in fact, a cow, and not instead a sheep, a bird, or a boy? The subsequent, more extended acts of denarration in *Molloy,* culminating in Moran's denial of the opening lines of his narrative, are implicit in this first textual undoing, as will be clear when I return to discuss this example at greater length below.

I term these negations "denarrated" descriptions and events, modeling my usage on Gerald Prince's concept of the "disnarrated," his term for possible events that, though referred to, remain unactualized in a text. Thus, in *Vanity Fair,* we find the following fateful nonevent: "If Rawdon Crawley had been then and there present, instead of being at the club nervously drinking claret, the pair might have gone down on their knees before the old spinster, avowed all, and have been forgiven in a twinkling. But that good chance was denied to the young couple" (146). Denarration, by contrast, would have affirmed Rawdon's presence in the company of Miss Crawley, and then denied this event.

We may identify a number of instances of this stratagem and go on to outline a kind of continuum of narrative negation; this will in turn enable us to specify the different functions it can have in the narrative world and the interpretation of that world. Near the end of Nabokov's *Lolita* Humbert writes, "Then I pulled out my automatic—I mean, this is the kind of fool thing a reader might suppose I did. It never even occurred to me to do it" (282). In *To the Lighthouse,* the irritable Charles Tansley is asked whether or not he is a good sailor. We are then informed that "Mr Tansley raised a hammer: swung it high in the air; but realizing that he could not smite that butterfly with such an instrument as this, said only that he had never been sick in his life" (91), as Woolf transforms a seemingly literal statement into a harmlessly metaphorical one. A comparable though rather more extended specimen can be found in Arnold Bennett's *The Old Wives' Tale,* where the narrator records the following speech: "'Yes,' said she. 'You can talk about your sister, and you can call *him* [by his first name], and you can mince up your words. But have you got a tea-service like this? . . . Did not my dress cost more than you spend on your clothes in a year? Has a man ever looked at you? . . ." (71). This passage is immediately followed by the disclaimer, "She did not say this aloud." There is nothing particularly revolutionary about these statements, but they do trespass slightly beyond the basic conventions of realism and point reflexively to the ways in which authors may modify, qualify, or negate material that had been presented as "given." Nevertheless, these will normally be processed by most readers as temporary, minor gaps that are resolved in the text almost as quickly as they are noticed.

For a more sustained and realistically motivated example, we may turn to Margaret Drabble's *The Waterfall* (1969). Well into the work we are informed by the narrator: "I told a really shocking lie at the beginning of this narrative, when I said that I told James I wasn't writing any more. . . . I lied, too, about the circumstances of Malcolm's departure. In fact I have already told two lies about this event, and who can tell if I will now risk a true account?" (130). This deceptively polymorphous novel starts off, as has been noted, narrated in the third person but, after 50 pages, the narrator switches to the first person in the name of a more accurate telling. A comparable situation occurs at the end of Ian McEwan's *Atonement* (2001) as the elaborate, emotionally satisfying resolution to the novel is revealed in the final paragraphs to have been a sustained fabrication, one that is more in line with poetic justice than the facts of the case. Most readers will probably grant these narrators the benefit of the doubt, and may even find a token of authenticity in the corrected representation of the narrator's erroneous path; the storyworld will remain stable as the transformation is limited to the narrator's act of storytelling. The contradictions can be explained epistemologically, as a function of the character of the two narrators, rather than as a postmodern overturning of the fictional world. At the same time, one is aware that with a few additional or more extreme interventions, the narrative world may start to fissure; instead of observing a fluctuating narrator alter descriptions of a stable world, we will see the world being created and re-created anew.

A playful, rather Shandyean admission occurs at the end of Rushdie's *Midnight's Children* (1980), as the narrator, Saleem Sinai, confesses: "I lied about Shiva's death. My first out and out lie—although my presentation of the Emergency in the guise of a six-hundred-and thirty-five-day midnight was perhaps excessively romantic, and certainly contradicted by the available meteorological data" (529). The first statement is a standard kind of denarration. The second sentence implies that Saleem's narration oscillates between mimetic and nonmimetic modes and contains a different kind of denarration. The endless night of the Emergency was not the literal darkness presented in the narrative but is instead merely a metaphorical figure to emblematize the excesses of that dark period. The literal, unrealistic meaning is negated by a statement affirming the figurative presentation of a historical event.[5] The boundaries between these poles are kept fluid, and narrative negation may be either a remaking of the narrative world or an invitation to read events metaphorically rather than literally. At this point we are still near the middle of the continuum though leaning decidedly toward the ontological slippages that, as Brian McHale has pointed out, characterize postmodernism; it is also here that the more extreme, destabilizing types of denarration begin to be found.

It will now be useful to return and further examine the dynamics of narrative negation in *Molloy.* After a vivid description of the moon that suggests temporal anomalies in the scene, Molloy goes on to write, "I say that now, but after all what do I know now about then, now when the icy words hail down upon me, the icy meanings, and the world dies too, foully named" (41). This claim is quite ironic, since if Molloy were genuinely unsure of what he remembered, he would have written his account in a more tenuous manner the first time. On the other hand, the comment does draw attention to the gaps, distortions, and fabrications inherent in any verbal reconstruction of the past. Other asides cast further doubt on the accuracy of the story being told: "She had a somewhat hairy face, or am I imagining it, in the interests of the narrative" (75). It is amusing to speculate on the kind of narrative such a description would enhance, even if we know in advance that it would doubtless be a rather Beckettian one. As the novel continues, more events are described, and more are called into question. Some qualifications refer to specific event descriptions: "But perhaps I am merging two times in one, and two women" (101), repeating the opening disavowal of the circumstances surrounding A and C. Other disclaimers more generally subvert the entire narrative: "and when I say I said, etc., all I mean is that I knew confusedly things were so, without knowing exactly what they were about" (118). In the end, all we can be sure of is that "what really happened was quite different" from anything we are told (119). This is true of the Moran narrative as well; despite its seemingly obsessive precision, it concludes with another act of denarration: "Then I went back into the house and wrote, It is midnight. The rain is beating on the windows. It was not raining. It was not midnight" (241).

Numerous other acts of denarration followed the publication of *Molloy* (1951). Some of the most explicit and radical have been discussed by Brian McHale in his analysis of what he terms "self-erasure" in postmodern fiction (99–106).[6] If one includes comparable cases of third person narratives that contain several contradictory events that are unresolved into any ontological hierarchy, the group becomes still larger. One can readily point to Robbe-Grillet's *Jealousy,* Robert Pinget's *Passacaille,* Raymond Federman's *Double or Nothing,* and Robert Coover's "The Babysitter." Other examples can be found with closer resonances to Beckett's texts, such as Robbe-Grillet's *In the Labyrinth* (1959), the beginning of which, as Richard Begam has pointed out (217n43), reads as a set of variations on the final sentence of *Molloy:* "I am alone here, under cover. Outside it is raining, outside you walk through the rain with your head down, shielding your eyes with one hand while you stare ahead nevertheless, a few yards ahead, at a few yards of wet asphalt; outside it is cold, the wind blows between the bare black branches. . . . Outside the sun is shining, there is no tree, no bush to cast a shadow, and you walk under the sun shielding your eyes with one hand while you stare ahead, . . . at a few yards of dusty asphalt" (141). At this point, I suspect we may be approaching the limits of the denarrated; no further or more thoroughgoing negation suggests itself as likely to be achieved.[7]

As noted above, these acts of denarration vary considerably in their overall effect on the stability of the represented world as well as on the reader's processing of the text. In the work of Bennett, Nabokov, and even Drabble, the denarration remains distinctly local, indeterminacies are temporary, and the stability of the represented world is not seriously challenged. In these cases, the narrators are simply modifying their stories, not reinventing the world they inhabit. This is partially true of Saleem Sinai's narration, which unfolds within a much less determinate ontology where fact and allegory, history and fiction, and the literal and the metaphorical regularly slide into one another; there is considerably less stable, determinate narrative there to be controverted. In Beckett and Robbe-Grillet, however, the denarration is global and undermines the world it purports to depict; very little (if anything) is left over after the assaults of textual negation the narrative performs upon itself.

One salient facet of these denarrated episodes is that they draw attention to what could be called, after J. L. Austin, the performative nature of the articulation of a fictional world. That is, if an omniscient narrator states that "Sitting beside the road, watching the wagon mount the hill toward her, Lena thinks, 'I have come from Alabama: a fur piece'" (3), this means, as we all know, that the transcription of the character's thoughts is *necessarily* correct; and this is, as Käte Hamburger and Dorrit Cohn have pointed out, one of the distinctive features of narrative fiction. It is also the case that everything else postulated by the narrator is equally true of the fictional world being depicted. In *Light in August,* in this part of the South, there is a road, there is a hill, Lena is sitting beside the road, and a wagon is coming toward her, she is heading toward a county named Yoknapatawpha. Unlike any nonfictional account of an arrival in some part of the South, once these words are written in a narrative fiction, they constitute some of the unalterable facts of its world. There is no way of falsifying these depictions by drawing on material outside the text, such as maps, atlases, or guidebooks. The only way they can be controverted is if the narrator disavows the statements at some later point in the work.

Intriguingly, this is also largely true of much first person fictional narration as well. If Marcel informs us of a certain event that took place in Combray, it is no good to say, as one might to an author of nonfiction, that when *Swann's Way* was published there was no such place as Combray, or that records of the period show no such person as Charles Swann, or that the dreams recounted sound as if they were invented, or that the events described form too perfect a symmetry to be entirely credible. We do expect a certain amount of what might be called "plausible fallibility" on the part of any narrator concerning the precise dates of private events, or any other act or event that depends on memory or involves judgment; in such cases, ordinary fallibility is a sign of verisimilitude. But in all larger, public areas, the first person narrator's word is definitive. To return to the example from Faulkner, the status of Yoknapatawpha does not change depending on whether it appears in a heterodiegetic or homodiegetic narration. In fictional first person narratives, the depiction of the fictional world is a constitutive act—whatever is said to exist thereby does exist. These basic facts of the textual world are simply given—but, once again, only as long as the narrator does not contradict them.

Naturally, such contradiction can happen, most obviously in the deranged or possibly insane narrators in many of the works of Nabokov; this practice can then call into question the reality of all the recounted events, and the reader learns this to be the case by observing salient indications within the text, usually involving contradictions in the recounting of key events or anomalies within basic interpretations. Thus, in *Pale Fire*, Zembla may possibly exist, or it may merely be a projection of the mad Professor Kinbote—unlike Combray, Hardy's Wessex, or Bennett's Five Towns, which are as real as the characters who reside there.

The denarrated in Beckett occurs in both his first and third person texts—not that he seems concerned to uphold that (or any other) boundary.[8] *Worstward Ho* presents a further, additional deployment of the denarrated, in which a world is slowly and painstakingly constructed as a number of fictional possibilities are stated and then immediately denied or revised to produce the most poetically bleak effect. "Say a body. Where none. No mind where none. That at least. A place. Where none. For the body. To be in. Move in. Out of. Back into.

No. No out. No back. Only in" (7). A page later we get the following revision: "Say ground. No ground but say ground. So as to say pain. No mind and pain? . . . Say remains of mind where none to permit of pain" (8–9). Denarration here happens phrase by phrase, and what is left unchanged does then take on a curious stability, though it is a distinctly provisional one.[9]

Eventually the shapes of the backs of a man and a boy appear; they are in the distance, poorly seen in the dim light, walking together but never receding (13). They briefly fade in and out of existence, returning unchanged (14–15). Then the man is depicted as kneeling: "From now kneeling. Could rise but to its knees. Sudden gone sudden back turned head sunk dark shade on unseen knees. Still" (16). This work is based on negation, and adding to the materials of the work is generally opposed: "Add others. Add? Never. Till if needs must" (25). As the work continues the outline of an old woman's head is grudgingly incorporated, as if to provide an observer. In the distance the two figures move apart; finally, they nearly disappear from the text: "Say child gone. As good as gone. From the void. From the stare. . . . Say old man gone. Old woman gone. As good as gone" (43). The denarration of the word of the text is concluded in its final paragraph: "Enough. Sudden enough. No move and sudden all far. All least. Three pins. . . . Whence no farther" (47). They are reduced to short, thin lines, in the "dimmost dim. Vasts apart" (47). Denarration here takes on the features of entropy, and all creation, all difference, slide into the void.

It is the first person form of the denarrated that is generally most prevalent and, I believe, more compelling. I suspect this is because it invites more possible interpretive positions concerning the subjectivity of the narrator, as the reader wonders whether the narrator is incompetent, disoriented, devious, or insane. And, when an especially contradictory line appears, it comically throws all of these conceptual frames into disarray, as the entire mimetic framework of the narration is abruptly called into question. At the very least, we may want to conceive of a new kind of fallible narration (postmodernism certainly has a way of expanding our sense of fallibility); the kind of figure we have seen employed by Beckett, Drabble, McEwan, and Rushdie might well be termed the "duplicitous" narrator, one, that is, who deliberately provides information that is later falsified by subsequent statements in the narration. This figure could thus be distinguished from two standard types of unintentional unreliable narrator that Dorrit Cohn has recently identified: the factually misinformed narrator and the "discordant" narrator who is ideologically biased or confused.[10]

Denarrated events pose yet another intriguing problem for narrative theory, specifically, how is one to separate story from discourse in a text like *Molloy*? If, as Rimmon-Kenan states, "'Story' designates the narrated events, abstracted from their disposition in the text [discourse], and reconstructed in their chronological order" (3), how are we to reconstruct any story when the discourse, as it unfolds, works to deny, negate, and erase the events recounted earlier? Instead of opposing a list of events from the reconstructed story to the sequence in which they are recounted in the discourse, there will not be much recoverable story at all, but rather a general, undifferentiated conglomerate of past events which may or may not have occurred, within an inchoate temporality that cannot be analytically reconstructed into any sustained order. All that is left for the narratologist to work with is the discourse, since all we know is the sequence in which the dubious events are presented or negated. At this point, a fundamental distinction at the foundation of modern narrative theory breaks down. Here, the usual separation between story and discourse collapses, and we are left with discourse without a retrievable story. The work's discourse is determinate; its story is inherently indeterminable.[11]

One point I wish to reemphasize here is the performative aspect of world making in narrative fiction, as well as the ontological destabilization always possible in fiction—a move that many postmodernists find irresistible. The play between narrative creation and destruction is typical of recent fiction as well as some earlier texts with anti-mimetic elements (e.g., *The Beggar's Opera, Jacques le fataliste*). We may also observe the ontological fragility of the status of much fictional discourse—at any point, the narrator can contradict what has been written, and thereby transform the entire relation between events as well as the way they are interpreted. Likewise, any third person text can become a first person text by a narrator's sudden self-revelation in the course of the fiction, as happens in Calvino's *The Nonexistent Knight* and several of the works discussed elsewhere in this book. Finally, denarration is also part of a larger kind of serious gamesmanship between the affirmation and denial of identities—individual, ontological, epistemological, or referential—and one that continuously reaffirms both the transformative and the disruptive power of the language of narrative.

III. The Permeable Narrator

Narration in the fiction of Samuel Beckett tends to revolve around two antithetical poles, both of which work to negate the basic epistemological drama of multiple narrators and focalizers with differing perceptions that animates most of the work of major modernists like James, Joyce, Broch, Faulkner, and Woolf. The first pole is solipsistic, as seemingly disparate narrative voices turn out in the end to be mere projections of a single isolated consciousness. *Company* (1980) is exemplary in this regard: it begins with the statement, "A voice comes to one in the dark" (7); much of rest of the text is an investigation of the nature, status, and identity of that voice. In the end, it turns out that "huddled thus you find yourself imagining you are not alone while knowing full well that nothing has occurred to make this possible" (61); the voice is not that of another, there is no one else. Such a failed attempt to generate "company" also appears in *Malone Dies*, "Cascando," "Not I," and other texts, narrative and dramatic, which follow the trajectory described early in *The Unnamable:* "I am of course alone. . . . I shall have company. In the beginning. A few puppets. Then I'll scatter them, to the winds, if I can" (292).

The other, opposite tactic is the uncanny and inexplicable intrusion of the voice of another within the narrator's consciousness. I call such a figure a "permeable narrator." Unlike the solipsistic gambit, which is readily situated within existing theories of narration, this other movement threatens to violate the principle of an autonomous, individual consciousness that is presupposed by all current theories of the narrator. To get a full sense of the force of this transgression, we may trace the emergence and development of the intrusive alien voice as it is played out in Beckett's trilogy.[12] In the first section of *Molloy*, Molloy occasionally hears voices; near the end of his stay with Lousse, he is afraid "of wearing out that small voice saying, Get out of here Molloy, take your crutches and get out of here and which," he adds, "I had taken so long to understand, for I had been hearing it for a long time" (59). Near the end of this section, Molloy notes that the voice had deserted him (87), but then he goes on to negate the reality of that voice: "every time I say, I said this, or I said that, or speak of a voice saying, far away inside me, Molloy, and then a fine phrase more or less clear and simple . . . I am merely complying with the convention that demands you either lie or hold your peace" (88). It would seem we are dealing with possibly nothing more substantial than a conventional depiction of the "voice" of the ego or even a conscience, and such depictions are themselves revealed to be entirely unreliable. We are given a bit of a twist then a couple of pages later when Molloy notes, "I heard a voice telling me not to fret, that help was coming. Literally" (91). It is not precisely clear what such a statement might mean, literally or otherwise, in such a dubious and self-negating discourse.

The voices that plague Moran in his narration in the second part of the novel are much less easily circumscribed. He begins by referring to a voice, which he is "only just beginning to know" (132), in the conventional terms of conscience with an occasional hint of an authorial muse, but very quickly describes it in quite different terms: "Yes, it is rather an ambiguous voice and not always easy to follow, in its reasonings and decrees. But I follow it none the less, more or less" (132). A few pages later we are informed of a most curious situation. Moran refers to "a rabble in my head, what a gallery of moribunds. Murphy, Watt, Yerk, Mercier and all the others. . . . Stories, stories. I have not been able to tell them" (137). This assertion overthrows the ontology of the work. Moran claims to have in his head voices of other characters created by Beckett—and in the case of Mercier, one inhabiting a text that had not yet been published. This ontological violation further problematizes the idea of voice: what can the source of such a voice be? Moran accepts it without comment, but later wonders about its nature and origin: "it was not so much Moran as another, in the secret of Moran's sensations exclusively, who said, No change, Moran, no change. This may seem impossible" (147). And, in all probability, it is. We are now far beyond the internalized speech of another, as found for example in the unsteady mind of the narrator of Dostoevsky's "Notes from the Underground." I argue that Moran is hearing an external voice, one that uncannily resembles or mimics the voice of his literary creator, impelling him onward. His mind is impregnated by the voice of another outside him. His final comment on the subject emphasizes the alterity of that discourse: "I have spoken of a voice telling me things. I was getting to know it better now, to understand what it wanted. It did not use the words that Moran had been taught when he was little. . . . But in the end I understood this language. I understood it, I understood it, all wrong perhaps. That is not what matters. It told me to write the report" (175–76). Moran's consciousness is now taken over and permeated by a voice that is not his own.

In the next volume of the trilogy, *Malone Dies*, we encounter a rather more realistic narrative situation, though it is one that reproduces many of the oddities of consciousness and narration present in more radical forms in the other volumes. Malone's mind is a bit strange; as he confesses, "the loss of consciousness for me was never any great loss" (183). He has the habit of turning external sounds into internal noises, and goes so far as to postulate that the various noises of the world have gradually "merged into a single noise, so that all I heard was one vast continuous buzzing" (207). There also comes a point where Malone transgresses the standard narrative situation in the most egregious manner. As Andrew Kennedy explains: "Malone-as-narrator is the controlling voice at all levels of narration, but his own 'authorial authority' is undermined at times. One of the most striking examples of such a radical device is Malone suddenly stepping out of the role of self-narrating narrator and seeing himself, in effect, as the creator of other characters in other Beckett fictions: 'Then it will be all over with the Murphys, Merciers, Molloys, Morans, and Malones'" (138).

Molloy's inner voice is readily reducible to his own subjectivity, while Moran's *daimon* is pretty clearly the speech of another. Malone's narration is entirely self-contained except for those uncanny references to other works by Beckett. The final volume of the trilogy, *The Unnamable,* takes this oscillation as the governing principle of its own extensive speculations on voice and narration. Indeed, the text starts off as a kind of mystery concerning the nature and identity of the narrator.[13] The narrator himself does not know what kind of space he occupies or how he got there; his earlier existence is opaque and he does not know whom he is speaking to; it is not even clear what kind of entity he is, or whether he is a single entity at all: "I seem to speak, it is not I, about me, it is not about me" (291). He spots a figure that appears to be Malone, though he quickly notes that it could be Molloy (292–93). His ontological status would thus seem to be that of an unfinished persona trapped in a limbo of characters, or else he is like an author, looking down on his creations, except of course they are not his but Beckett's creations. He goes on to assert the contradictory claims that "Basel and his gang" (including the other characters?) are "all lies . . . all invented, basely, by me alone" (304) as well as admitting:

> It issues from me, it fills me, it clamors against my walls, it is not mine, I can't stop it, I can't prevent it, from tearing me, racking me, assailing me. It's not mine, I have none, I have no voice and must speak, that is all I know, its round that I must revolve, of that I speak, with this voice that is not mine, since there is no one but me, or if there are others, to whom it might belong, they have never come near me, I won't delay to make this clear. (307)

At one moment the narrator takes credit for all the other voices in the narrative; at the next he complains he is at their mercy. He claims both to be outside his narrative and imprisoned within it. This dilemma is not easily resolved, as the two opposed positions collapse in on one another. Basil is rechristened Mahood, and the narrator states that "his voice continued to testify for me, as though woven into mine, preventing me from saying who I was, what I was" (309). New variables enter this bizarre drama of identity and nonidentity, as basic narrative relations of distance, priority, hierarchy, existence, self, and other are raised and then utterly obscured. Every conceptual opposition, every statement of difference, is immediately collapsed or negated. The notion of the self is entirely undermined, and Descartes' *cogito,* as David Hesla (1971) points out, is controverted by the Unnamable (114).[14]

As the narrator states, "It's entirely a matter of voices, no other metaphor is appropriate. They've blown me up with their voices, like a balloon, and even as I collapse it's them I hear. Who them?" (325). In its starkest form, the basic question remains: is the voice internal or external? If external, what is its possible source: "Who them?" If internal, is it a projection or delusion, or is it the voice of another character speaking through him due to his internalization of the other's speech? Then again, is it somehow both internal and external at the same time, say a preternatural voice sounding within him, *daimon*like, or is it the voice of an author creating and directing the thoughts of the narrator? Or is one speaker simply making all the voices up? All of these hypotheses are plausible, yet each is contradicted at many points by some aspect of the other possible answers.[15]

As the narrative continues, the paradox of its speaking grows more intense and its resolution seems more intractable: the narrator wonders whether what is required is "praise of my master. . . . Or the admission that I am Mahood after all and these stories of a being whose identity he usurps, whose voice he prevents from being heard, all lies from beginning to end. And what if Mahood were my master?" (311). This contradictory welter of possibilities does not suggest any unproblematic way out of the conundrum, as what seem to be other characters and narrators go on to merge with the Unnamable. After all, it was Mahood "who told me stories about me, lived in my stead, issued forth from me, came back to me, entered back into me, heaped stories on my head. . . . It is his voice which has often, always, mingled with mine, and sometimes drowned it completely" (309). Every possible relation between Mahood and the narrator are assayed; none is able to be confirmed or refuted.

The self-referential interrogation pauses as the narrator assays more descriptions, offers some partial memories, and tries out a few abortive stories. The book emerges as one of the most defiantly anti-narrative works ever composed, in which all the basic elements of storytelling are negated. There is no determinable temporal or spatial setting, no characters to speak of, no events worth narrating, and no clear audience or motive for the narration. The main engine of the text is the compulsive voice that will not stop, and the primary drama of the text is the determination of the identity of the narrator and its voices. We are teased by the question of whether the speaking "I" creates or belongs to the world of the fiction. Numerous passages suggest that both are in fact the case, one of the more insistently paradoxical of which may be cited:

> No one left, no one to talk to, no one to talk to you, so that you have to say, It's I who am doing this to me, I who am talking to me about me. Then the breath fails, the end begins, you go silent, it's the end, short-lived, you begin again, you had forgotten, there's someone there, someone talking to you, about him, then a second, then a third . . . then they depart, one by one, and the voice goes on, it's not theirs, they were never there, there was never anyone but you, talking to you about you, the breath fails, it's nearly the end, the breath stops, it's the end, short-lived, I hear someone calling me, it begins again. (394)

As the narrative winds down, there are no more breaks between sentences, the voice becomes less aggressive, the other figures melt away, and closure beckons. At this point the Unnamable makes rather more admissions than usual that all the others are his creation: "there was never anyone, anyone but me, anything but me, talking of me to me, impossible to stop" (395), and "I've always been here, here there was never anyone but me, never, always, me, no one, old slush to be churned everlastingly" (403). Passages like these have helped lead a number of critics to conclude that this work too, like many of Beckett's other texts, is ultimately a vain attempt by an isolated consciousness to engender some solace, company, or identity. This position is most succinctly put forth by Linda Ben-Zvi (1986): "'I' talking to 'you' about 'me,' the tripartite form of the self doing battle against the unnamed 'they,': that is the final image of *The Unnamable* and in many ways the ironic image that lurks behind all Beckett's fiction. A self that is split, talking aloud, trying to coalesce and to continue against the 'they' that thwart it" (100).[16]

But Beckett does not attain resolution so easily. The narratological analysis I have undertaken here suggests exactly the opposite conclusion. Every identity is dissolved and every hierarchy subverted; each claim that the voices are all invented is repeatedly followed by counterclaims of the insistence of an external voice. "It's not I, that's all I know, it's not mine" (414). The speech of the primary narrator merges with that of the temporarily internal narrators; it is not always clear who invented whom: "And another question, what am I doing in Mahood's story, and in Worm's, or rather what are they doing in mine" (377). We have another set of references to other works of Beckett, rather more ambiguous, if possible, than the earlier ones in the trilogy: "All these Murphys, Malloys, and Malones do not fool me. They have made me waste my time, suffer for nothing, speak of them when, in order to stop speaking, I should have spoken of me and me alone" (303). The Unnamable here seems to be impersonating an overly simple version of Beckett himself, as he muses on the inability of his earlier creations to express that which can only be delivered by the unusual, disembodied narrator of this text. How can this unreal narrator know of Beckett's other books? It is only by a metaleptic framebreaking that allows him to be outside the textual world he otherwise often seems to inhabit. We may grant that the Unnamable can invent all the other figures and even the voices, but he can't have invented Beckett's other creations as well. This kind of threshold crossing reveals the impossibly protean nature of the "dis-framed" narrator and shows that there remains a fundamental alterity that cannot plausibly be reduced to any single consciousness. In the words of Richard Begam, "Beckett succeeds in collapsing the narrator/narrated into an undifferentiated third term, the mediating slash that formerly stood as the sign of demarcation but now disperses itself into an interstitial zone" (156).[17]

In the final pages of the text the question of interiority is explicitly invoked: "it's an image, those are words, it's a body, it's not I, it wouldn't be I, I'm not outside, I'm inside, I'm in something, I'm shut up, the silence is outside, outside, inside, there is nothing but here, and the silence outside, nothing but this voice and the silence all round" (410). Here too we see not the reduction of the external to the internal but their repeated collapsing into one another as indeterminacy and fragmentation reign. "I'm there somewhere, it won't be I, no matter, I'll say it's I" (410). There is no resolution to the question of the identity of the narrator; he remains to the last a contradictory conflation of self and other, essence and absence. In the words of Angela Moorjani, the labyrinthine "prison of textual duplication, of doubling and redoubling fictions, of lying images and voices . . . is being sabotaged by the textual play. The narrator attacks the 'hell of stories' by subverting narrative discourse from within" (60).

§

As might be expected, this text plays regularly with the nature and function of the narrating pronoun and utilizes a considerable number of divergent perspectives. The narration opens with a self-conscious first person voice, "I, say I" (291), moves quickly on to self-narration in the second person, "You think you are simply resting" (291), and then concludes that the third person "it" form is most appropriate: "It, say it, not knowing why. . . . ," explaining, "I seem to speak, it is not I" (291). The text goes on to oscillate between more standard first and third person narrators, though the normal status of each is invariably undermined: "They say they, to make me think it is I who am speaking. Or I say they, speaking of God knows what, to make me think it is not I who am speaking" (370). Over halfway into the text, another narrating possibility is briefly assayed: "let's drive on to the end of the joke, we must be nearly there, and see what they have to offer him, in the way of bugaboos. Who we? Don't all speak at once" (360). This begins as a rhetorical "we," but the attention called to it makes one wonder as to its actual status. Such curiosity is immediately dashed by the speaker: "no sense in bickering about the pronouns and other parts of blather. The subject doesn't matter, there is none" (360). This last statement may well be literally true.

Later, after a long passage that once again conflates and deconstructs discreet narrative and narrating agents, the voice attempts to get to the root of the confusions: "you don't know why, you don't know whose, you don't know against whom, someone says you, it's the fault of the pronouns, there is no name for me, no pronoun for me, all the trouble comes from that, it's a kind of person too, it isn't that either, I'm not that either, let us leave all that" (404). The oddity of a first person speaker claiming "there is no name for me" is dwarfed by the even stranger denials throughout the text that the speaker is not an "I," from the opening paragraph's "I seem to speak, it is not I" (291) to the protestation on the final page: "it's not I, that's all I know" (414). In between we find numerous, additional declarations of the inaccuracy of the "I": "I shall not say I again, ever again, it's too farcical. I shall put in its place, whenever I hear it, the third person, if I think of it" (355). Even in denying the "I" an "I" is invoked, but the "I" is largely evacuated of any identity or essence. It is, in the end, merely a decentered text saying "I." Or in the words of the Unnamable, "who is I, who cannot be I, of whom I can't speak, of whom I must speak" (404). Beckett is here explicitly and repeatedly assaulting the conventions of all traditional narration that demand a story be told in either the first or the third person, as well as the entire critical and theoretical corpus that, since Percy Lubbock, has acted as if these are the only possibilities in fiction. Instead, *The Unnamable* provides one of the most extreme, fascinating, and outrageous demonstrations of the possibilities of narration in—and only possible in—a work of fiction.

The permeable narrator has had a significant career during the course of the twentieth century. It begins with the wandering thoughts of one character that inexplicably wind up in the minds of another in *Ulysses* as mentioned in the introduction, and the many bleedings of one consciousness into the thought of another in Borges ("The Circular Ruins") and Beckett ("here long silence, there will be no more I, he'll never say I any more . . . he won't think any more, he'll go on, I'll be inside" [*Fizzle* 4]). *The Unnamable* remains a kind of fountainhead of the most extreme kinds of permeable narrators, as figures on the same ontological level are fused and then separated back out. It also presents a related "dis-framed narration" where larger narrative levels are collapsed together metaleptically. Permeable narration would go on to become a favorite technique of the authors of the *nouveau roman* in their more extreme experiments, such as Robbe-Grillet's *La Maison de rendez-vous* and *Project pour une révolution à New York,* Robert Pinget's *Le Fiston* and *Passacaille,* and Claude Simon's *Les Corps conducteurs.* It also figures prominently in postmodern novels such as Raymond Federman's *Double or Nothing* (1971), Christine Brooke-Rose's *Thru* (1975), Juan Goytisolo's *Paisajes despues de la batalla* (1982), and Rushdie's *The Satanic Verses* (1988). This practice is perhaps the most thoroughgoing negation of the humanistic concept of a narrator who is like a person, since it violates what is probably the most important aspect of personhood, which at least since Descartes has been conceived of as a mind. When that mind is contaminated by debris of another, the very possibility of a unitary self is exploded. All of these works deserve to be better known and would repay a sustained narrative analysis, not along traditional lines but the kind made possible by the concept of the permeable narrator.

IV. Postmodern Unreliability

We need to directly address the question of narratorial reliability in contemporary fiction. Despite impressive recent studies on unreliability, culminating in James Phelan's astute analysis of six types of unreliability (*Living* 49–65), additional work is needed to encompass the more extreme kinds of unreliability postmodernism delights in producing. Summarizing and extending the findings of this study, we may identify and bring together the varieties of posthumanist narrators and voices that have superseded the traditional figure of the narrator as a person who is telling a story and who is subject to the normal abilities and limitations of a human being or humanlike narrating agent.

1) The Fraudulent Narrator. Unreliability has proliferated under postmodernism, and we need some new concepts to add to current notions of unreliable and untrustworthy narrators. One avowedly anti-mimetic construct that is needed may be designated the "fraudulent narrator": for a paradigmatic case we may cite the obvious anachronisms of the narrator of Charles Johnson's *Middle Passage* (he refers, for example, to Piltdown Man eighty years *before* the hoax was concocted). Another instance would be the eleven-year-old narrator of John Hawkes' *Virginie: Her Two Loves.* In a typical passage, she writes: "Did I dream the darkness that wears soft the stone, like sheep in the narrow passages of a labyrinth? (The darkness that changes in density and moves, magnifies the smallest sound, and lives so curiously alive yet unsatisfyingly between the sleeper and all the activity he awaits in the sun.)"(34). There is no pretense of any mimetic illusion here; no one will believe for a moment that an eleven-year-old, no matter how precocious or poetic, could have penned such words. Hawkes is flouting the realistic convention that a character narrator should seem to write the way such a figure could be expected to in the real world, and thereby perhaps critiquing such ineffective illusionism which invariably produces, in the hands of Henry James, a governess that writes unbelievably like Henry James.

Fraudulence comes in many forms, and we will want to specify its more interesting varieties. We begin with the relatively unobtrusive (and rarely remarked on) type found in *Molloy.* Its narrator is so befuddled that when asked by a policeman to produce his papers, he merely pulls out the bits of newspaper he uses to wipe himself with. And yet this same narrator is capable of referring to the doctrines of the minor philosopher Geulincx and observing lyrically, "all I know is what the words know, and the dead things, and that makes a handsome little sum, with a beginning, a middle and an end as in the well-built phrase and the long sonata of the dead" (31). Another kind of fraudulence is what Ann Jefferson has called the *invraisemblable* in the work of Sarraute: "the narration of *Portrait d'un inconnu* repeatedly transgress[es] the realist limitations of the narrator's position in order to give an account of the inner lives of the other characters. Indeed, most of the novel's major scenes are based on such transgressions" (120–21).

An opposite kind of fraudulence is found in the case of a clearly unbelievable narrative that a narrator somehow is able to credit for a time. In Borges' "The Immortal" (1949), the narrator of the preposterous first person inner story (who claims to have spoken to Homer and drunk from a fountain of youth) discovers that he is not merely unreliable, but impossible: "The story I have told seems unreal because the experiences of two different men are intermingled in it" (193); that is, the narrator, in recounting his life story, has conflated it with another's. The framing material at the end of the text resolves this anomaly: the tale does not, in fact, entwine the lives of disparate individuals within the spurious identity of a single "I." Instead it is revealed that the narrator is simply a deluded fabricator, writing a fiction in the first person that he originally believes to be an autobiography, and then equally erroneously supposes is the story of an "I" and a "he." As we will see in the next chapter, fraudulent narrators also figure prominently in contemporary drama.

Other important anti-mimetic narrators include 2) Contradictory Narrators. In Robbe-Grillet's *La Jalousie,* Robert Coover's "The Babysitter," and J. M. Coetzee's *In the Heart of the Country,* multiple, contradictory versions of what are presumably the same events are set forth, with no mechanism offered (such as different narrators with different memories and agendas) to explain away the often outrageous contradictions. Using naturalistic assumptions to comprehend these texts leads directly to interpretive chaos; one must abandon the idea of a self-consistent narrator relating an account of a preexisting set of events to begin to read these unusual pieces. This too represents a kind of unreliability unimagined in current narratology.

3) Permeable Narrators, as we have just seen, are distinct figures who merge and blend into one another without any signal or expla-

nation, and are thus a large-scale extension of vagrant thoughts of one character that somehow find their way into the consciousness of another as noted above. The impossibly straying thoughts may be relatively isolated, as in the case of *Ulysses,* or occupy large chunks of the entire narrative, as we find in Claude Simon's *Les Corps conducteurs,* Juan Goytisolo's *Paisajes después de la batalla,* Robert Pinget's *Le Fiston,* and of course *The Unnamable.*

4) Incommensurate Narrators, as discussed above, are those who cannot be the single source of the heterogenous voices of texts they seem to narrate. As Monika Fludernik states, "neither a story and/or common situation nor a group of consistent characters nor even a consistent narratorial voice can be projected from 'stories' like Donald Barthelme's 'You Are as Brave as Vincent van Gogh'" (*"Natural"* 287–88). The heterogeneity of the materials thus must exceed our ability to postulate a single, realistic consciousness responsible for all of them. Earlier in this chapter and elsewhere in this book, I suggest that this approach is particularly useful in designating the protean figure(s) behind the most contradictory acts of narration in *Ulysses.*

Finally, we may identify 5) Dis-framed Narrators, who move from one level of a text to another in ways that are impossible outside of fiction. Thus, Moran, the narrator of the second part of *Molloy,* claims to have invented characters that appear in other novels by Beckett. The most tersely expressed articulation of this condition is the statement uttered by (and about) one of Christine Brooke-Rose's narrators: "Whoever you invented invented you too" (*Thru* 53).

Unnatural Narration in Contemporary Drama

chapter six

On- and offstage narrators have occupied prominent positions in the drama for most of the twentieth century. Among the many such figures, one may point to the protagonist of O'Neill's *The Emperor Jones* (1920), the Voice in Cocteau's *La Machine infernale* (1934), and the Stage Manager in Wilder's *Our Town* (1938). Since narration in drama is not known as well as it might be, I will start by describing a common instance, that of Tennessee Williams' *The Glass Menagerie* (1945).[1] It is a partially enacted homodiegetic narrative in which the narrator is also a participant in the events he recounts and enacts. At the beginning, an actor comes on stage, identifies himself as "the narrator of the play, and also a character in it," sets the scene ("I turn back time"), and describes the other characters and the concerns of the play. He indicates that what is to follow is a memory play and observes that, consequently, it is not realistic. Here the diegetic portion ceases and the mimetic part begins, as what was uttered by a single, governing voice becomes enacted by several speaking characters. Later in the play, the protagonist resumes his functions as narrator to introduce the third and sixth scenes, and to comment on the action in the fifth scene. At the end of the performance, he narrates the gist of his subsequent travels and brings the story up to the time of its telling. The stage directions also encourage variation in this figure's performance to enhance its effect: "The narrator is an undisguised convention of the play. He takes whatever license with [mimetic] dramatic convention is convenient to his purposes" (22).

Another major presence and subsequent source for many later strategies of narration is the drama of Bertold Brecht. In his essay "Theatre for Pleasure or Theatre for Instruction?" (1935–36), Brecht outlined the distinctive features of the epic theater he created, stressing the use of narration: "The stage began to tell a story. The narrator was no longer missing" (71). Not only did Brecht employ narrators in many of his plays; he also displayed written texts before each scene that frequently had a narrative function. In *The Caucasian Chalk Circle* (1944), a bard is actually brought on stage to narrate a story. In doing so, he generates a fictional world in a manner similar to that of an omniscient narrator. Brecht's storyteller narrates diegetically, in the third person, until, pointing to the stage, he directs actors to mimetically enact the narrative he is recounting. This oscillation between the two representational modes then continues throughout the play. In contrast to a standard memory play like Williams', this type of work is a heterodiegetic narrative in which the narrator resides in an ontologically distinct level from that occupied by the characters. Other generative narrators include the Stage Manager of Wilder's *Our Town* (1938) and, more radically, the storytelling characters of Milan Kundera's *Jacques and His Master* (1981).

Postmodern inversions of the conventional onstage narrator can be quite striking. In David Henry Hwang's *M Butterfly* (1989), we find instances of permeable narration as the thoughts and memories of the narrator, Gallimard, are contaminated by another. The character Song even insists that certain past scenes be set forth despite the fact that he himself is merely a memory in the consciousness of another. Confronted by this strange demand, Gallimard protests, "You have to do what I say! I'm conjuring you up in *my* mind" (78). Tom Stoppard's *Travesties* (1975) dramatizes the memories of an old man, Henry Carr, who is growing senile and whose recollections are at times wildly inaccurate. At other points, his memory is impossibly, indeed "fraudulently," accurate, as when he recalls James Joyce composing works that he has never read, or "remembers" Russian dialogue spoken by Lenin. This extreme unreliability and the "fraudulent" narration are further blended with highly stylized representations, as when the character Joyce regularly speaks in limericks. The framework of the memory play is thus in Stoppard's hands largely a pretext for its parodic violation.

Fraudulent narration is also a major factor in Paula Vogel's *The Baltimore Waltz* (1992), a drama in which the main characters narrate and enact a trip to Europe. It is, however, a very strange trip: the secondary characters resemble figures out of European *films noirs* and other popular media rather than actual people one might encounter in contemporary France, Holland, or Austria. A waiter speaks in a thick "Peter Sellers French" accent and another figure called The Third Man also narrates and acts out melodramatic scenes. We finally learn that the trip was never taken, and that its episodes are imagined events inspired by old movies and set in a fictional Europe. Together, the three plays just mentioned present one person's memories contaminated by another, an incorrectly remembered past, and fabricated accounts of travel that never occurred.

As might be expected, one of the most compelling dramatists to employ narration on stage is Samuel Beckett, especially in his later work, where dramatic narrators and monologists create the world around them as they name it (e.g., *A Piece of Monologue* [1979]). Most apposite for the purposes of this study is Beckett's 1963 radio play, "Cascando." A narrator called "Opener" begins the play, calling on secondary figures "Voice" and "Music" respectively to recount a tale of the hapless movements of a figure called Woburn and to produce appropriate melodies in counterpoint to the embedded narrative. Opener proceeds in total mastery of the two subordinate figures until part way through the piece, at which point both begin to weaken and fade. Like many of the narrators of Beckett's fiction, Opener insistently affirms the independence of the other figures, vigorously denying that they are merely internal creations of his own: "They say, He opens nothing, he has nothing to open, it's in his head" (*Plays* 140). As the play continues, Opener's control weakens further; he even becomes afraid to open. Nevertheless, he perseveres, and with increasing difficulty is able to get the other progressions back in motion. Finally, all sound ceases, as the halting movements of Woburn, the desperate narration of Voice, the failing music, and the vain attempts of Opener to go on all come to a halt. By the end, it seems clear that the other figures were indeed all in the head of the fatigued Opener.

Another device that has proven most apt for dramatic experiments in narration is the offstage voice. Unique to performance is the disembodied narrative voice that sets the stage, comments on events, and propels the action.[2] The first examples I will set forth are heterodiegetic ones, though homodiegetic cases can also exist; in this area, theatrical options resemble those of the voice-over in cinema. The Voice in Cocteau's *The Infernal Machine* (1934) is a representative example: omniscient, ironic, and interventionary, it informs us at the beginning of the second act that it will wind back the clock and represent other events unfolding at the same time as those that have just been displayed. In *The Singular Life of Albert Nobbs* (1977), Simone Benmussa starts with an offstage representation of the voice of George Moore, the author of the story the play is adapted from. Actors then appear and dramatize the story he has begun to tell; throughout the production, he will also provide various narrative asides. Hélène Cixous, in *Portrait of Dora* (1976), further extends the subjectification of the narrative voice, as an entity referred to as "The Voice of the Play" draws attention to slippages of identity in the drama and the impossibility of determining what actually happened, as opposed to what was desired, projected, transferred, or misremembered.

A still more radical transformation appears in Marguerite Duras' *India Song* (1972). This work contains four offstage voices which usually comment on or inquire about the events being enacted on stage. At other times, however, their comments permeate, take the place of, or echo the characters' dialogue; sometimes, they even seem to engender the next sequence of actions. It is a shifting, unstable relation that re-creates and relativizes the offstage voice in new ways. As Elin Diamond has observed, "though the stage enactment seems to emerge from the memory of the voices, the voices are incapable of assuming a stable narrating position; rather they react fearfully, helplessly, anxiously, erotically, both to what they witness and what they partially remember" (102).

This narrative fascination is so complete that the voices' interactions constitute a second, offstage drama that is both parallel to and dependent on the play enacted on the stage, as the voices speak for the actual audience and at other times seem to usurp the prerogatives of the author. They dislodge the fixity of critical categories grounded in mimetic assumptions, as memory and invention, narration and description, seeing and speaking glide into one another. Sarah Kozloff, in her study of the subject, has suggested that voice-over narration in film humanizes and tames an otherwise "odd, impersonal narrative agency" (128). I argue that in the plays just described the opposite is the case, as offstage voices work to decenter identity and defamiliarize conventional practices of dramatic representation.

Tom Stoppard has also shown how thoroughly voice-over in a video medium can be destabilized. His 1984 television play, *Squaring the Circle,* is a kind of postmodern documentary about the events surrounding the Solidarity union in Poland during 1980 and 1981. It pushes the generative narrator to new extremes by applying the technique to historical events that were largely unknowable at the time of its filming. It has a narrator, whose role at first seems to be merely that of the conventional pseudo-objective voice-over. Soon, however, the voice contradicts the enacted events. After introducing Brezhnev and Gierek talking together on a beach at a resort on the Black Sea, the narrator goes on to state that "This isn't them, of course." In close-up we then see the (suddenly) bodied narrator who, looking directly into the camera, continues speaking, "and this isn't the Black Sea. Everything is true except the words and the pictures. If there was a beach, Brezhnev and Gierek probably didn't talk on it" (21–22). The deceptively omniscient documentary voice is here demystified and revealed to be a single, situated speaker with his own positionality and limited knowledge. The drama also includes a character identified as the Witness, who explains many of the issues to the narrator and at times corrects him and criticizes his presentation of images (pp. 54, 66–67, 78, 82). The potentially authoritative voice that most documentaries strive to achieve is thus individualized, democratized, and shown to be fallible. What is ultimately contested here is nothing less than any claim to the epistemic privileges of heterodiegetic discourse (such as omniscience), at least in genres like the documentary that purport to be nonfictional.

Contemporary dramatists transgress mimetic conventions of narration in still other ways, as our last examples will disclose. Pinter's *Family Voices* (1981) consists of three voices—those of a mother, father, and son—that seem to be reading aloud letters they have sent each other; as the play progresses, it becomes apparent that the mother's letters have never been read; the son's never sent (and probably never written); while the third set are voiced by the father, who is dead and is literally speaking from beyond the grave. The work, though first broadcast as a radio play, is regularly presented in "platform performance" in which the physical proximity of the actors speaking the texts intensifies the unbridgeable ontological chasms between the characters even as it underscores the rhetorical failure of these "letters" as forms of human communication.[3]

Beckett's later short play, "Not I" (1972), as its title suggests, also interrogates self and identity in addition to any traditional, fixed narrative stance. The work consists primarily of a torrent of words that are uttered by a single illuminated mouth, an arrangement that draws considerable attention to the nature and function of this strange, nearly disembodied voice. The drama is what I have called in Chapter One a "pseudo–third person" narration, as the mouth sets out a sad account of the miserable existence of someone identified merely as "she." But this attribution is illusory; the jumbled narrative refers not to another, but rather the speaker herself. Mouth's truncated and repetitive life story is, however, so wretched that the speaker refuses to acknowledge any connection to it, despite reiterated promptings by another voice that only she can hear. This strange communication adds to the epistemological drama of the work, as the audience, like Mouth, struggles to identify and keep distinct the various subjectivities that are invoked, as the following selection should suggest:

> back in the field . . . morning sun . . . April . . . sink face down in the grass . . . nothing but the larks . . . so on . . . grabbing at the straw . . . straining to hear . . . the odd word . . . make some sense of it . . . whole body like gone . . . just the mouth . . . like maddened . . . and can't stop . . . no stopping it . . . something she—. . . something she had to—. . . what? . . who? . . no! . . she! . . . (*Plays,* 221)

We find, that is, a mélange of description and narration, invention and memorial reconstruction, and self-correction and the contradiction of another (internal? internalized?) voice.

To add to this rich confusion of subjectivities, there is also the physical presence of another, silent figure, dressed in black, on stage as well. Even after we solve what might be called the modernist riddle of the work, i.e., that the "other" described in the third person is actually a displaced version of the self that speaks, the postmodern enigma remains: just who or what is Mouth, and to whom (or what) is she speaking? Numerous possibilities suggest themselves, many of which are reminiscent of the questions posed by the Unnamable: she may be an image of a madwoman, a figure in hell, an allegory of the dispossessed, or a parody of authorial creation; she may be addressing the imagined voice of another, another version of herself, or the metadramatic image of a stage prompter. But more than anything else, the very physicality of this staging of a contaminated consciousness—the disembodied mouth and the unexplained auditor—ensures that no critical gesture will be able to unify these defiantly inorganic fragments.

Paula Vogel's *Hot 'n' Throbbing* (1993) is one of the most innovative and powerful developments of several of the strands of narration and subjectivity that have been traced above. There are two primary figures in the play, a woman who is trying to scrape together a living by writing erotic film scripts for a feminist film company, and her former husband, a physically abusive man who, drunk, breaks down her door as she is working at her computer. There are also two "permeating" narrative voices: one, designated the "Voice-Over," is female, a kind of muse, the woman's inner voice and source of the narrative material that the woman types; it is also, at other moments, a voice of temptation, of her feminist conscience, and of the language of horror films. The other, called "Voice," is a protean male discourse that uses a number of styles and accents, speaks in male clichés, proffers diagnoses in the language of early sexology, and reads out phallocratic passages from figures like D. H. Lawrence, Henry Miller, and Nabokov's Humbert Humbert. Its different voices form a collective social discourse of male domination and control.

As if this were not experimental enough, Vogel pushes the medium still further: both voices are literally embodied on the stage: the playing space is dual, at once an ordinary living room and at other times a fantasy erotic dance hall, and the voices in the former space are physically present—that is, portrayed by actors—in the latter. Here, Voice-Over is also a sex worker, located in a glass booth where she dances during the play. The Voice is also corporeally present as the owner/bouncer of an erotic dance hall, acting "like a live DJ, spinning the score of the piece" (232) and often breathing heavily into his microphone. At times, he also sounds like the abusive husband. No wonder the protagonist asks in an aside after a passage of fallacious, turn-of-the-century sexology is uttered by the Voice, "Where is that coming from?" (249).

As will be readily imagined, the drama is as much about the struggle between two competing narratives as it is about the individuals who happen to speak them. This discursive clash occurs in seemingly minor areas as well as in those of mortal significance. As the woman, Charlene, sits at her computer and tries to come up with synonyms for "throbbing," Voice-Over proffers "pulsating" and "heaving," while Voice in turn suggests the more violent "beating" and "battering" (243–44). The play also documents the circulation of public discourses about gender and sexuality, as speeches and ideas overheard or adapted by the woman are incorporated into her text, and will presumably go on to animate other individuals who will view her film once it is finished. Here, a creative, nonviolent recursivity is offered as an alternative to the more deeply ingrained narrative and behaviors of the culture at large.

At the end of the play, individual acts of discursive resistance are overwhelmed by male agencies of institutional control. Voice, now taking the role of a film producer, demands that the script be inverted so that the woman in it is bound and helpless. On the other set, the abusive man gains physical control of the situation, and proceeds to batter and finally kill his former wife. In this final scene, the two characters lip-sync the almost predictable words of contemporary domestic violence that are provided by Voice and Voice-Over, as the man acts out the savage social script he knows so well.

Narration has long been a basic feature of the twentieth century stage, and many basic concepts of narrative theory can be enhanced by reference to approximate equivalents in performance. Questions such as those concerning the status and gender of otherwise unmarked narrators are clarified (or intensified) when the voice that speaks the lines is male or female. Issues of focalization can be nicely complicated when we are presented with a full staging of the protagonist's consciousness—or told, as we are in *India Song,* that the voices now "see" the action on the stage. A number of Bakhtinian concepts take on greater immediacy by reference to their theatrical incarnations, such as polyphony or interior polemical speech, when the disparate or conflicting voices within a single consciousness are spoken by different actors. Even the narratee becomes more complex when he or she is present on the stage, or gestured to in the audience. One hopes for more studies of narration in the corpus of authors who, like Beckett or Duras, experiment with voice in both fiction and drama.

The pieces I have discussed above, in addition to providing extensions and reinventions of the figure of the narrator, also share in modern literature's continued transgressions of conventional boundaries as well as its general dissolution of the notion of a unified individual consciousness. They dramatize distinctively postmodern types of extreme narration by employing what I have termed fraudulent and permeable narrators and, in the case of Vogel's Voice, an incommensurate narrator. They also display a contemporary take on the intersubjectivity and even intertextuality of the self—the way individuals are constructed by the discourses that surround them—and foregrounds the play with voice and narration, which regularly fragments and recombines the subjectivities it cannot resist interrogating. Like contemporary fiction, modern drama has for some time transcended the simple, humanist narrator figure and has gone on to create "unnatural" narrators who exceed and subvert the limits of an individual consciousness.

Implied Authors, Historical Authors, and the Transparent Narrator

TOWARD A NEW MODEL OF THE NARRATIVE TRANSACTION

chapter seven

Having examined a wide array of narrators, acts of narration, and authors as characters, we may now move on to reexamine all the elements of the standard model of the narrative transaction, or the movement of the text from its origins in the author to its reception by the reader, familiar to students of narrative theory from Seymour Chatman's revision (151) of Wayne Booth's earlier model:

[Real author] → Implied Author → (Narrator) → (Narratee) → Implied Reader → [Real reader]

We'll start with the concept of the implied author, which has unexpectedly become a site of recent debate. A number of eminent narrative theorists, most prominently Gérard Genette (*Revisited* 135–54) and Ansgar Nünning, have called for the rejection of the concept of the implied author as unnecessary for narrative theory, and Mieke Bal has little use for it (119–20).[1] Michael Toolan, writing from a linguistics-oriented position (77–78), likewise avers that the implied author is not a real role in narrative transmission (though he grants it is a real position in the reader's processing of the narrative, "a projection back from the decoding side, not a real projecting stage on the encoding side" [78]). Others have vigorously argued for the utility of the concept, most notably William Nelles ("Implied"), Susan S. Lanser ("(Im)plying"), and Wayne Booth ("Resurrecting"). The most thorough and comprehensive recent defense is that of James Phelan (*Living* 31–65). The debate shows no signs of letting up; still more discussion is, I believe, very much in order. In this chapter I will examine both the strongest evidence in favor of the case for the implied author as well as the reasons behind the desire to do without the construct. I argue that we can find a number of cases where its use is indispensable, though we will also find cases where it is not necessary at all. This paradoxical concept is thus often but not always essential. In addition, an adequate model for implied authors and other narrating voices will suggest a very different picture of the narrative transaction from the way in which it is usually conceived.

In what follows, I will be referring exclusively to a streamlined version of the original concept as articulated by Wayne Booth: the implied author is the figure constructed by the reader of the person who produced the narrative, and who may differ significantly from the actual flesh-and-blood author. In Gerald Prince's summary of this position, the implied author is "the implicit image of an author in the text, taken to be standing behind the scenes and to be responsible for its design and for the values and cultural norms it adheres to" (42).[2] Thus, one may confidently speak of the implied author of *Tom Jones* as being genial, ironic, easy-going, and magnanimous, without going to biographies of Henry Fielding to ascertain whether the historical author actually possessed all of these qualities as well. Without consulting historical accounts, one will never know whether or not the actual man was often petty, unforgiving, improvident, prickly, cheap, or obtuse when it suited him; one does know, however, that the implied author of *Tom Jones* is none of these things.

It should probably not be surprising that the idea of the implied author arises in the wake of literary modernism (and, for that matter, complements the related notion of the unreliable narrator). In *Contre Sainte-Beuve,* Proust clearly articulates the modernist concept of the author: "A book is the product of a different self from the one we manifest in our habits, in society, in our vices" (99–100). In a late diary entry Virginia Woolf would similarly muse on how each book of hers "accumulates a little of the fictitious V.W. whom I carry like a mask about the world" (*Diary* 5, 28 July 1940, 307). Indeed, the difference between implied and historical authors can be so great that it has given rise to stories about the incommensurability between the two, most dramatically in Henry James' "The Private Life" (1892).

Real authors may, as Booth notes, create implied authors who are more admirable than themselves: this is most obviously the case in the more self-serving autobiographies. The opposite can also occur. Certainly, some rather tame writers infatuated by the tradition of the *poet maudite* must have made their implied authors much more wicked than the authors themselves ever dared to be in society; Lord Byron was demonstrably more cheerful than the world-weary implied author of *Manfred.* Another interesting correlative of this position is that an implied author can appear more progressive ideologically than his or her real life counterpart. Faulkner's implied author was more liberal on race matters than was the private individual, who notoriously cautioned African-Americans to "go slow, now" in attaining basic civil rights; Joyce, though often dismissive of women he encountered, nevertheless produced texts that give voice to women's concerns in a manner that two generations of feminist critics have found to be salutary.

Real and implied authors can differ in still more fundamental ways: As William Nelles has pointed out, the implied author of the novels of George Eliot is male, and this fact caused much consternation among her readers ("Implied" 27–29);[3] David Carroll notes, "when her pseudonym was lifted shortly after her first novel appeared, many readers felt they had been badly deceived: the clerical gentleman who stressed so impressively the demands of duty in his vivid picture of a Christian society turned out to be a female atheist living with another woman's husband" (2, quoted in Nelles, "Implied" 27). We may go further, and observe that the implied author of *Don Juan* gives every indication of being heterosexual, society's default category, though the historical Byron often enjoyed the embraces of young men.

Other indisputable cases of significant differences between the actual and the implied author include forgers and ghostwriters, as even Genette was forced to admit (1988: 146). Concerning forgers and fraud, the erudite historical MacPherson was obviously utterly different from the anonymous medieval bard he invented in *Ossian,* and the Southern white segregationist author (Asa Carter) is notoriously different from the Native American implied author ("Forrest Carter") he fabricated in the pseudo-autobiography, *The Education of Little Tree.* Phelan astutely points out that in a different kind of hoax, as that perpetrated by Alan Sokal on the editors of *Social Text,* "the real author constructs an implied author who actually closely shares her beliefs, attitudes, and values but who seems sincerely to espouse quite different ones. [Thus,] unsuspecting readers, especially those who share the values the implied author is pretending to espouse, are likely to be taken in" (*Living* 46).

The job of political ghostwriters is to sound like the politician they write for, providing that the politician has a distinctive voice at all; if not, it is to impersonate the more resonant features of the person's previous ghostwriters. The dangers of fabricating a voice for another are illustrated by the case of Thomas Mallon, the unlucky journalist who ghostwrote the autobiography of the blundering Dan Quayle. As Joe Queenan observed, Mallon's literary talents far outstripped the Vice President's, a man "widely perceived to be a nincompoop." Thus,

> If Mallon wrote a book that was too lofty and cerebral, it would make Quayle seem like a cheater and a fake. But if he wrote a book that was indefatigably dopey, it would make it seem like he was merely cashing a big paycheck. . . . Wisely, Mallon [chose to arrange] Quayle's banalities in a lucid, plausible sequence that made the author seem neither terribly smart nor terribly dumb. . . . Mallon probably achieved the ghostwriter's overarching objective: producing a book that sounds like something the author could conceivably have written if only he had the time. Say 400 years. (8)

We may move on to discuss some cases in which two or more actual human beings produced a fictional text that was intended to be received as if it had been written by a single individual. What should be a classic scene in this debate are the early pages of the fifth chapter of the second part of *Nostromo,* including the arch conversation between Martin Decoud and Antonia Avellanos, which were written in the hand of Ford Madox Ford. When it appeared, no one ever suspected the chapter might not be the work of Conrad. Later, it was learned that Conrad was very ill and unable to complete this installment for magazine publication. Ford, his friend, neighbor, and collaborator on three other volumes, visited his ailing colleague and picked up the pen. Whether Ford took Conrad's dictation, developed some sections that Conrad could not complete, or wrote it all himself will never be known (though the scholarly consensus seems to suggest a rather substantial contribution by Ford). This is because the text so perfectly reproduces Conrad's characteristic tone, style, and concerns that it seems as if a single author wrote it. And in the end, that is basically what the implied author is. The pages in question are now regularly included in the collected works of both authors.

Many other examples of less celebrated authors come readily to mind. If a prolific writer of detective novels dies before his or her popularity wanes, it does not mean that the flow of books will soon cease. Any unfinished, partially written or merely outlined books are quickly turned over to a ghostwriter—all too apt a term in this context—who then completes the works in progress, writes up the ones in outline, and even creates new ones "in the spirit" (pun intended) of the deceased author. In some cases, new books are written over a decade after the literal death of the titular author. I suggest that from a narratological or interpretive perspective, books may well be properly published under the name of the dead author as long as they strongly resemble in significant ways the other work of the same implied career author. And in the publishing world, these books likewise tend to be successful only insofar as they mimic the voice and reproduce the characteristic features of the deceased author. Other media provide many more examples: as Chatman has observed, folk ballads have multiple actual authors, and the cluster of writers who produce a Hollywood screenplay do so by attempting to make the work seem as if it were composed by a single sensibility (149); typically, the film is a critical failure when competing visions jar perceptibly and inharmoniously—whether or not they were written by the same physical individual.[4]

Genette is wrong to maintain that the texts of jointly authored works never "betray the dualness of their authorial agents" (*Revisited* 147).[5] It is often the case that we detect different implied authors in texts. This is one way we uncover plagiarism in and assign authorship to biblical passages. Even if we did not have prior knowledge that Guillaume de Lorris's *Roman de la Rose* was completed by Jean de Meun, we would certainly detect the pronounced shift in tone, subject matter, and purpose. A similar (though less pronounced) disjunction is said to occur between the original eighty chapters of Tsao Hsueh Chin's *The Story of the Stone*, and the final forty chapters, which were written by an anonymous, inferior author who altered the design of the work.[6] There is no need to run a computerized analysis of the syntax and vocabulary of *Pericles, Prince of Tyre*, to readily know which portion was written by the anonymous journeyman and which was done by Shakespeare. And in the case of the ruined film, we know at what point the craven producer decided to have the ineluctably tragic ending replaced by a sentimental one, thus giving its implied author an irrevocably split personality. The examples from the last few paragraphs show that two authors of a single work may retain their separate authorial identities, or they may fuse into the figure of a single implied author.

This kind of analysis can even be extended to popular music: in most of the Beatles' songs, a single implied creator seems to be behind the words and music. In some, we feel the predominance of Paul ("Michelle"); in others, John ("Lucy in the Sky with Diamonds"). "A Day in the Life," however, seems like two different songs by different sensibilities grafted together in a way that cannot be explained even by its allusions to mind-altering drugs. The mystery vanishes once we discover that Paul and John met one day in the studio, each in possession of half a song which they then proceeded to run together. Once apprised of this fact, many listeners report that they understand this curious song much better.

Another series of works will prove pertinent to this discussion: books written by several authors, each of whom is responsible for a chapter or other such unit. The preeminent example is a book called *The Whole Family* (1907–8), a novel that relates its narrative from the perspectives of twelve first person narrators, each of whom is a family member or friend. The first chapter was written by William Dean Howells in his characteristic tone, style, and sensibility, though with rather less verve than usual. The second, however, by Mary Wilkins Freeman, displays an ironic and even acidic tone, an irreverent set of motives, and a series of outrageous disclosures that so differed from the first chapter that it threatened the continuation of the project. As Alfred Bendixen recounts in his introduction to the volume, Freeman "made the old-maid aunt into a thoroughly modern woman who relished the attention of men. . . . The quiet world Howells had created in the first chapter was shattered by Freeman's revelations that the young man who had just become engaged to the daughter, Peggy, was really hopelessly in love with the aunt" (xii). As can be readily imagined, such transformations threatened the identity of the work: Howells loathed Freeman's chapter and urged the editor, Elizabeth Jordan, not to publish it, pleading: "Don't, *don't* let her ruin our beautiful story!" (xxiii). The other contributors likewise refused to alter their authorial personae; as Jordan would recall, "Almost every author seemed to consider the chapters before his merely as material leading up to his own work, and to judge it solely in relation to his individual plans" (Bendixen, xxvi). Needless to say, Henry James' narrator's contribution reads just like Henry James, and contemporary reviewers noted how oddly it was situated between the discordant voices that preceded and followed it.[7]

Here we have a dozen implied authors of a single narrative. When the work was first published chapter by chapter in serial form, the individual author of the piece was not identified. Instead, the names of all the contributors to the project were listed with the admonition, "The intelligent reader will experience no difficulty in determining which author wrote each chapter—perhaps" (cited in Bendixen, xxxv). When the work appeared in book form, each author's contribution was clearly identified. By contrast, a very different intent was behind a modern version of the same experiment in collective narration, *Finbar's Hotel,* devised and edited by Dermot Bolger, in which each author is attempting to submerge his or her own style and sensibility into that of a single implied author.[8] In between these two extremes, we may situate a recent issue of the *Paris Review* (Volume 164, Winter 2002–3) in which eight contemporary novelists including Michael Cunningham and Jonathan Franzen collaborate on a murder mystery. The identities of each distinctive contributor can be derived using the same technique necessary to solve the murder in the story.

There is one more possibility to discuss: that of the single individual who writes in different voices to impersonate distinct authorial selves. Jasper Milvain writes two anonymous reviews of the same book for publication in two different magazines in George Gissing's *New Grub Street* (1891). "You wouldn't suspect they were written by the same man, eh?" he asks his sister, and is delighted when she confirms he has successfully disguised (or is it multiplied?) his authorial identity (443). Some contemporary authors have attempted to produce a comparable effect, incorporating various documents into their texts that either were or seem to have been written by someone other than the author (for example, the indigenous text that runs through Nadine Gordimer's 1974 novel, *The Conservationist*).

In a similar vein, we can reflect upon the multiple discursive standpoints in *Ulysses,* including those we have just examined in "Ithaca," that have driven its critics to come up with the notion of the "arranger" (see Hayman 88–104). Joyce's practice goes beyond the multiple narrators that come from the single, magisterial implied author of *The Waves* or *The Sound and the Fury.* For Joyce critics, it has proven nearly impossible to reconcile the Flaubertian intelligence behind the first nine chapters with the various extreme anti-Flaubertian sensibilities inferable from many of the later chapters, which are not only distinct from but antithetical to the earlier part. As Karen Lawrence notes, "in 'Eumaeus,' Joyce chooses the 'wrong' word as scrupulously as he chooses the right one in the early chapters" (167). I believe, as I argued in the last chapter, that we can better circumscribe the work by thinking of *Ulysses* as having more than one implied author. I understand very well that many readers will not want go along with this interpretation: after all, one author wrote the entire book; why can't we then construct an implied author that does the same, it will be objected. The case may become clearer with what seems to me an irrefutable example, that of Chaucer's retraction of the *Canterbury Tales*. There is no good reason to doubt that the historical author who wrote the "Prologue" and "The Tale of Sir Thopas" also penned the final note that renounces the entire work. But clearly this must be a different implied author, specifically, one who denounces and retracts all the brilliant, ribald humor of the implied author of the rest of the book. This ideological negation is, I suggest, comparable to the aesthetic antinomy Joyce produces in the oddest episodes of *Ulysses*.[9] The example of Chaucer, at least, should reveal that a single work by a single author can produce two implied authors, just as stylistically or aesthetically autonomous parts of works written by different historical authors can produce different implied authors.

These examples should show conclusively that the notion of the implied author is a coherent and useful one for a wide range of critical practices, and there is no reason to discard this concept, which, as we have seen, cannot be reduced to other authorial or textual functions. Nevertheless, several qualifications are in order. Though the construct has a distinct use, is it always necessary to the analysis of a fictional work? Here the answer is "no." The more formulaic a work is, the less of a need there is to account for an individuated authorial voice; that is, no distinctive author is properly implied by such novels. Second rate mysteries, Harlequin romances, and pornography—and for that matter, most Restoration comedies—exhibit no distinctive authorial presence, unlike the considerably more individualized works of Dashiell Hammett, Georges Bataille, or William Congreve.[10] It is also the case that the notion of the implied author is of considerably less relevance for writers of satire, allegory, apologue, or authors like Voltaire who are much more interested in conveying ideas than in manipulating narrative techniques (including voice). The closer the thesis of a work of fiction is to the other writings and public behavior of an individual, the less need there is to invoke an intermediary figure to situate between the person and the book. The same is also true of aesthetic statements or programs that are both articulated and embodied within a text.

Here too, the criterion of falsifiablity is our best guide. If one were to object to Balzac that there was no such person as Rastignac or that Paris in the 1840s was rather different than it is described in his novels, he could rightly claim that such "objections" are not applicable to a work of fiction. But if one objected that money or passion are not actually the driving forces that shape human behavior as presented in his novels, he might well reply instead that you do not understand human nature nearly as well as he does. That is, such claims could be falsifiable, and thus reproduce the thought of the author.[11]

Wayne Booth, who invented the concept of the implied author, also set forth the notion of the "career implied author," which most subsequent theorists have, perhaps wisely, chosen to ignore.[12] Intuitively, we might well find this concept both useful and quite odd. If it is limited to works of fiction, why form a composite picture of all the implied authors of the writer's novels but exclude our picture of the person who wrote the essays, letters, prefaces, and other nonfictional prose? It is also odd to use an idea of a career implied author that cannot cover the full career of many authors, but instead more accurately designates stylistic shifts or "periods" in the author's work that are perfectly understandable when viewed together. On the other hand, there is often a consistency of style, voice, and themes in a given author's mature work that justifies an overarching concept like this one: before the identity of the writer was known, readers and critics had no trouble referring to "the author of *Waverley*" as the novels seemed to come from a single hand; not a few (including Jane Austen) suspected that the career author Walter Scott, who had never before written a novel, might well be responsible for these works. This concept is essential when historical scholars attempt to attribute anonymous pieces to known writers; think only of the assembling of the corpus of Daniel Defoe. It is also implicit, I think, in the phrase, "Here's another Agatha Christie—You'll love it!" That presupposes a large, reliable set of similarities from book to book, some of them distinctive. It may be granted that, when discussing the work of a novelist like James who has left a large body of nonfiction, the "career implied author" of the fiction tends to merge readily into the notion of the actual author who wrote the prefaces, essays, and autobiography. Nevertheless, in other cases the concept is quite distinct and demonstrably useful. A particularly compelling example can be found within the "Wakefield" cycle of mystery plays. Some of these anonymous works are written in a distinctive style and voice that scholars have long identified as belonging to the "Wakefield Master"; in this case, textual evidence alone impels us to construct a single implied author (whose works, for all we know, might actually have been composed by a brother and sister, or a husband and wife) to explain these consistent individuating features.

This phenomenon is also present in adjacent arts: we may correctly identify a piece of music we have never heard before as a work of Beethoven, and we know what kinds of things to expect when we are about to view a previously unseen Monet. Cinema has the concept of the *auteur* to designate the distinctive markers of a director's style and vision. We may also note that the pseudonym is a classic method employed by an actual author to create a different implied author; thus, Kingsley Amis used the name Robert Markham to write James Bond novels that were much closer in style and sensibility to the fiction of Ian Fleming than to those of the author of *Lucky Jim*. There are also many notorious cases where a major rupture exists between the earlier and later career of an individual such that it is not clear that the notion of a single career author is useful at all to depict such a heterogenous output; this is especially relevant for authors who have undergone a conversion experience and dismissed or renounced many of their earlier productions (Tasso, Tolstoy, Aragon, Sollers). Intriguingly, this is also true of authors that take time developing a distinctive voice or have trouble maintaining it.

Here too, Conrad provides an interesting case study. Conrad's first novel, *Almayer's Folly,* does not quite strike the distinctive note he would soon attain. He even dismisses his early story, "The Lagoon," as "a tricky thing with the usual forest river-stars-wind sunrise, and so on—and lots of second hand Conradese in it. . . . Upon my word I hate every line I write" (letter to Garnett, 14 Aug 1896, *Collected Letters* 1, 302). Soon after writing these lines, Conrad entered his major phase, producing the work his reputation would rest on. By 1915, however, many of his short stories, admittedly written for ready money, often approached the status of "second hand Conrad"; still more sadly, Conrad's final novels did not begin to approximate the work of his earlier self. That is, by the time he was writing *The Arrow of Gold* (1919), Conrad could not imitate his earlier form nearly as well as Ford Madox Ford seems to have done. At this point, Conrad is literally no longer the career author he once was. The case of the decline of Hemingway is still more dramatic. As Nelles points out, "an author may parody his or her own work, creating two implied authors that correspond to a single historical author. One might read such a parody, albeit unintentional, in some of Hemingway's late work such as *Across the River and Into the Trees*" ("Implied" 41–42)—to say nothing of the posthumously published manuscripts which the historical author wisely kept locked in his drawer. It seems to me that we are justified in retaining the concept of the career implied author as being of some definite critical utility, referring to a different career implied author only when it becomes an authorial persona that is difficult to square with its earlier avatar. This may be predicated of radical stylistic shifts as well as ideological ones: the mature Byron and perhaps the later Yeats are vastly different figures than their earlier literary selves despite a number of significant features in common.

Interestingly, postmodernism often produces an opposite effect: as narrator after narrator is discarded or undercut or revealed to be a fabrication, the novelist thereby produces his or her most characteristic effects. This is most obviously the case with someone like Beckett, whose series of narrational trap doors and false starts, as we have seen, are a characteristic feature of the career implied author. This paradox is further exemplified by Calvino, who in *If on a winter's night a traveler* includes the following statement: "So here you are, ready to attack the first lines of the first page. You prepare to recognize the unmistakable tone of the author. No. You don't recognize it at all. But now that you think about it, who ever said that this author had an unmistakable tone? On the contrary, he is known as an author who changes greatly from one book to the next. And in these very changes we recognize him as himself" (9). Calvino's characteristic tone is a playful, ironic, self-referential one, fully present even (or especially) in lines where he denies its existence. This is the Calvino we all recognize.

A curious feature of most existing notions of the implied author is the fact that this concept, as usually formulated, does not allow for the theoretical possibility of actual authors ever speaking directly to any audience even if they want to. They may do so in a preface, but once the fiction starts, the implied author and narrator take over and the actual author may not speak. No one would hesitate to refer to the ideas of an author of a critical essay, but when the same ideas appear in the story proper, the words are attributed to the narrator and the concepts merely to the implied author. This is a very strange arrangement, especially since some authors write books to express ideas, while others, like Oscar Wilde, will take epigrams uttered by characters and narrators in his works of fiction and republish them as nonfiction. Tolstoy's reflections on history in *War and Peace* likewise were extracted from the body of his text and printed as an epilogue; later they were published as a pamphlet of nonfiction. We should note here that philosophical or other general statements are portable into and out of narrative fictions in a way that specific characters and events typically are not. Seymour Chatman takes the position that brackets the world from the text in its most extreme form when he affirms that it makes no sense "to hold the real Conrad responsible for the reactionary attitudes of the implied author of *The Secret Agent* or *Under Western Eyes* (or, for that matter, Dante for the Catholic ideas of the implied author of the *Divine Comedy*)" (149). This seems to me to be palpably false, and would have seemed so to the historical Dante as well, I'm sure.

This situation leads to another example, that of Fielding, in Book III chapter vii of *Tom Jones,* "In which the Author himself makes his Appearance on the Stage," as the chapter heading puts it. The text states:

> Prudence and circumspection are necessary even to the best of men. . . . It is not enough that your designs, nay your actions, are intrinsically good; you must take care they shall appear so. . . . Let this, my young Readers, be your constant Maxim, That no Man can be good enough to enable him to neglect the Rules of Prudence; nor will Virtue herself look beautiful, unless she be bedecked with the outward Ornaments of Decency and Decorum. And this Precept, my worthy Disciples, if you read with due Attention, you will, I hope, find sufficiently enforced by Examples in the following Pages. I ask pardon for this short appearance, by way of chorus, on the stage. . . . this, as I could not prevail on any of my actors to speak, I was obliged to deliver myself. (v. I. 140–41)

My question is, Why must we treat this passage as the exclusive work of a narrator or, following Booth, an overt implied author? Can it not also simply be, as Fielding would have it, the words of the author that appear in the novel proper? The same words written in a preface or afterword would be called the discourse of the author; why must we deny this as a theoretical possibility just because the words appear within the part of the book designated as fiction? If not, we are forced into the very odd position of having to say that the narrator is impersonating the historical author. If we do that, what then are we to do with the self-conscious statements about the organization and techniques of the book which prove to be accurate, or, at a still more personal level, with that speaker's references to Fielding's family? Genette is right to observe that "when the narrator of *Tom Jones* makes one or two references to his deceased Charlotte, he is indeed signing himself Henry Fielding" (*Revisited* 144). It seems to me that a theory that cannot admit this as a theoretical possibility is needlessly impoverished. (This is of course assuming that the words in the novel do in fact correspond to the author's novelistic practice, aesthetic design, and general worldview as articulated in his or her nonfiction—a judgment that can only be made after the relevant nonfictional sources are consulted.) It should also be acknowledged that our notion of the historical author is a mediated figure that we construct out of a diverse body of sometimes incompatible textual sources; my point is not that it isn't a construct, rather that it is a different kind of construct made up of different materials and subject to different rules of reception.[13]

It is evident that, in cases where there is no need to evoke an implied author, the source of the narration must rest either with the narrator or the author. In such accounts, we find yet another compelling instance of the move to revive the figure of the author, long pronounced dead by poststructuralist authorities, but recently resurrected in a number of guises by theorists as diverse as Ross Chambers, Eugen Simion, and Paisley Livingston. A particularly telling example can be adduced from the work of Voltaire. A modern biographer has stated that *Candide* contains all of Voltaire's "ideas, eccentricities, and tics; it even includes his answer to Rousseau's letter on providence." He concludes that "no book has ever been so completely the image of [the mind of] its author" (Orieux 314–15). Here, there is no need to invoke any implied author, and no function for that concept to perform. In an apologue, whether Voltaire's, Samuel Johnson's *Rasselas,* or Plato's allegory of the cave in *The Republic,* the ideas expressed are simply those of the author.

James Phelan has recently argued that an accurate account of the implied author must disrupt the neat symmetry of Booth's and Chatman's models of narrative communication; Phelan is right in this approach. Extending this position further, I suggest that we need to alter our basic model of the narrative transaction from the symmetrical series of boxes within boxes deployed by Chatman in his extension of Booth's original diagram, and replace it with a model of variable, irregular ellipses that can touch one another's boundaries at points.

I offer three such examples in figure 2, each modeling a different kind of narrative. In the case of Voltaire, the implied author is generally so close to the actual author (and, for that matter, to the narrator)

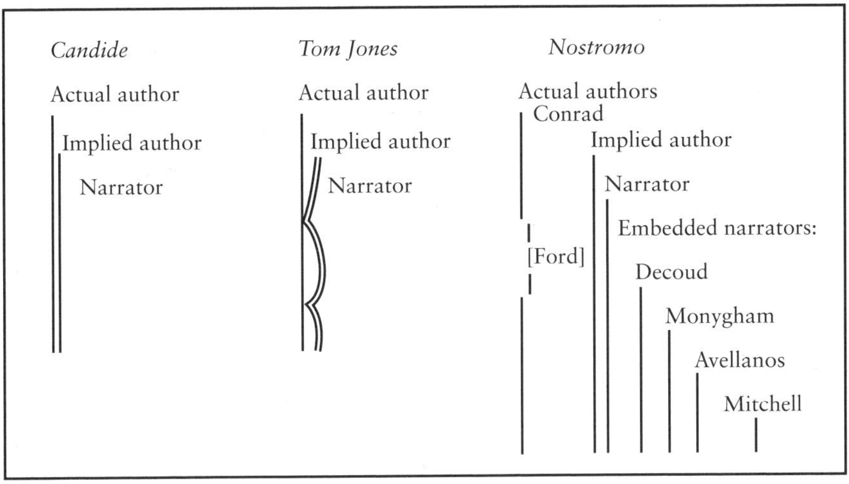

Figure 2. Actual and Implied Authors and Narrators in Three Texts

that there is little need for any additional category; the implied author may largely be equated with the historical author with little or no loss, practical or theoretical; we would need only a double line to designate all three of the potentially different figures or voices that are undifferentiated in this text. The narrator and the author are the same in autobiography; the same is often true of apologues. In the case of Henry Fielding, there is little practical need to sandwich an implied author between the actual author and the narrator, even as we acknowledge that historical and implied authors may be quite proximate though not identical at every point. As we have seen, there is always a gap or fissure between even the closest cases of near identity between author and implied author, if only that the implied author is invariably more consistent than the actual author ever is. Nevertheless, the very proximity between the two causes Booth to seem to conflate these figures in *The Rhetoric of Fiction,* where he says that Fielding's "second self" or implied author "is given an overt, speaking role in the story" (71). For nearly all other writers on the subject, only a narrator speaks, while the implied author is the inferrable mind behind the text, or in the resonant phrase of Nelles, the historical author writes, the implied author means, and the narrator speaks ("Implied" 22). I suspect it is in practice very difficult to construct an image of the author from the text *without* including the discursive comments of the narrator as long as they are entirely consonant with everything else in the book—events, moral, aesthetics, and ideology. As Booth states, "our picture of [the implied author of *Amelia*] is built, of course, only partly by the narrator's explicit commentary; it is even more derived from the kind of tale he chooses to tell. But the commentary makes explicit for us a relationship which is present in all fiction" (73).

A very different set of relations is at work in *Nostromo*. Here, we have two historical authors collaborating to produce a single implied author whose calm Olympian detachment and imperturbable pessimism are quite different from the harried, strained, and often exhausted Conrad or the reckless and improvident Ford; indeed, Ford notes that a violent attack of gout and nervous depression—qualities unimaginable in the implied author—forced Conrad to ask for assistance. The implied author in turn is distinct from the primary third person narrator as well as the curious voice that speaks as "we" partway through the text. These in turn are vastly different from the various internal narrators who provide highly mediated and typically distorted accounts.

Though the implied author is often quite close to the narrator in much third person fiction, a number of prominent exceptions to this general practice can be found. In Thomas Mann's *Death in Venice*, the implied author is considerably more tolerant of homosexual desire than is the queasy narrator, as Dorrit Cohn has masterfully shown (*Distinction* 132–49). It is also the case that the implied author never questions for a second the heteronormative world he inhabits, unlike the historical author, whose homosexual experiences were among the most profound of his life. Indeed, the difference between the historical and implied authors can be measured by the shock that was felt by many when it was learned that the creator of the story was so different from its implied author.[14] Margot Norris (216–36) has likewise shown how the third person narrator of "The Dead" reproduces the sensibility and prejudices of its primary focalizer, Gabriel Conroy, even as the implied author plies the text with material that resists the shared perspective of protagonist and narrator: the "lyrical narrative voice is not 'innocent' but rather produces a fair share of male 'palaver.' . . . Joyce therefore repeatedly nudges us to think against the ideological grain of the narration by genderizing ourselves . . . as subjectively female" (217).

It is important to observe that these relations are variable, not fixed; we need to acknowledge a most important strategy that may be termed the "transparent voices phenomenon," in which the most unreliable internal narrator can readily (and, more importantly, incontrovertibly) articulate the ideas of the author. In such cases, the narrator may be temporarily "emptied" and his character dispensed with as the author speaks directly and sometimes incongruously through that character's mouth. Think of Humbert Humbert's distinctly Nabokovian contempt for psychoanalysis, mass culture, socialist realism, and American philistinism, which are expressed in language more reminiscent of Nabokov's nonfictional prose than they are of Humbert's other beliefs and idiosyncrasies.

Intriguingly, the author's voice even breaks through the second-rate mind of the fatuous John Ray, the otherwise utterly fallible editor of Humbert's text. Consider Ray's reference to "old-fashioned readers who wish to follow the destinies of 'real' people beyond the 'true' story" (6), or the following more tongue-in-cheek intrusion: "The commentator may be excused for repeating what he has stressed in his own books and lectures, namely that 'offensive' is frequently but a synonym for 'unusual'; and a great work of art is of course always original, and thus by its very nature should come as a more or less shocking surprise" (7). These sentiments are the kind frequently stated in Nabokov's critical prose and far beyond the reach of a middlebrow psychiatrist who, to be more in character, might say instead that all great books are sincere and teach important lessons—to note only two conventional platitudes repeatedly excoriated by the master.

Likewise, in *Don Juan,* the historical author, the implied author, and narrator are all entirely co-extensive when the narrator denounces tyranny, mocks Christianity, satirizes English society, deplores Wordsworth, argues for Greek independence, or calumniates Byron's ex-wife (who appears very thinly disguised as Donna Inez in Canto I). We may note that Milton approximated this device for his own subversive ends and was able to articulate many of his anti-royalist sentiments by placing them within the discourse of Satan in *Paradise Lost.* The "transparent narrator" is a favorite technique of postmodern authors, who regularly use it to transgress the carefully maintained ontological boundaries observed by realist and modernist writers.

On the other side of the narrative transaction we find an equally ungovernable cluster of narratees and implied and actual readers. These normally distinct figures can fuse or multiply in different kinds of narrative. In a work like *Pilgrim's Progress,* the narratee is the implied reader, and the implied reader is intended to be a model for all historical readers (though, of course, he isn't). Similarly, what Robyn Warhol has termed "the engaging narrator" communicates directly

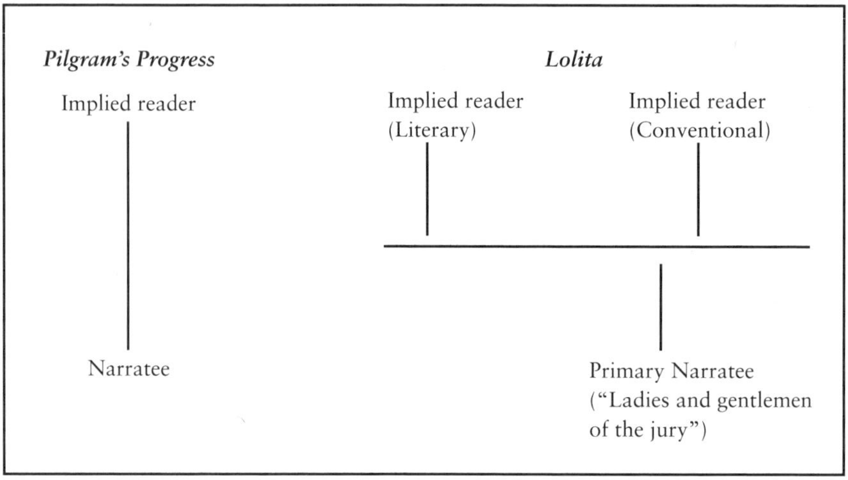

Figure 3. Implied Readers and Narratees in *Pilgrim's Progress* and *Lolita*

with the actual reader, thereby cutting through the divisions that an excessively formalist position would seek to impose: "Writing to inspire belief in the situations their novels describe[,] these novelists' used engaging narrators to encourage actual readers to identify with the 'you' in the text" (29).[15] And as we noted in Chapter Two, the autotelic form of second person narration regularly fuses the narratee and the actual reader.

These figures can also multiply; just as there may be several narratees in a work, some authors write for two or more different implied readers or "authorial audiences," to use the terms of Peter Rabinowitz, who has shown how this is done in Nella Larsen's *Passing,* a text directed to both those who are able to perceive its lesbian subtext and to those who cannot. We may find a number of dual implied readers in African American fiction and in modernist narratives.[16] I have argued elsewhere that Conrad's "Heart of Darkness" and "The Secret Sharer" both seem designed to be read by two incompatible audiences, one more conventional, the other more skeptical ("Conrad and the Reader"). A text like *The Whole Family* will have many more implied readers.

The chart in figure 3 illustrates the possible range of actual readers, implied readers, and narratees in two works familiar to students of narrative theory. (I do not include a place for actual readers since they cover all possible positions of reception.) *Lolita* seems to be addressed both to an authorial audience that gets all the ironies and allusions and also to a more middlebrow reader whose expectations are frustrated at every key turn of the narrative, as I have discussed elsewhere (1997). The implied reader or authorial audience is at times much less a universal figure than was once imagined; it is often or even typically gendered (think of Hemingway's implied reader) and otherwise delimited in a historically determined manner.[17] The resisting reader, as Judith Fetterley calls her, should also be acknowledged in the narrative transaction even if a more proximate place for her has been precluded by the narrative texts themselves.

It will be readily apparent that the two halves of the narrative transaction, as I have depicted them in the diagrams above, do not match up together well at all. The left side will never correspond systematically or even approximately to the right side. My only defense to this gross violation of the order, precision, symmetry, and simplicity of existing models is that the ones offered here, in all their Shandyean detours and divagations, are ultimately more comprehensive and more accurate for dealing with the notorious waywardness of narrative fiction. We may also, it turns out, discover an unexpected connection at the furthest edges of this now rather messy set of figures: as Robyn Warhol and others have noted, serial fiction allows for the possibility of the desires of the readers to affect the turn of events between installments of the work; the reader thus becomes a collaborator in the authoring of the narrative in a much more literal way than that ever suggested by Barthes in his notion of the writerly text. A similar case could be made for the reader of a hyperfiction, where the reader determines the narrative by selecting from among a number of plot options provided by the author.[18]

The distinctions discussed above are extremely important but need to be depicted rather differently from the standard "Chinese box" model. I would rather see a few different diagrams. One would be a spectrum with actual author on one side and implied author at the other. A corresponding spectrum of implied author and narrator would also be most useful. It is here that many central interpretative battles are fought, often under another name: any interpretation of a number of potentially ambiguous or contested works turns on just how close the narrator is to the implied author, as is evidenced in texts like "The Prioress' Tale," *The Man of Sentiment, A Portrait of the Artist as a Young Man,* and *The Good Soldier,* while in other texts such positions fuse or interpenetrate, as most vividly demonstrated in Borges' mobile conundrum, "Borges and I."

In summary, I wish to affirm the following points: 1) the implied author is a coherent and useful concept that can be applied to many works of fiction and is essential in discussing modernist works. 2) A work of fiction can have more than one implied author. 3) The implied author is not, however, an indispensable aspect of the narrative transaction and has no real place in a number of didactic, allegorical, or apological works. 4) The concept of the implied author is not necessary for every work of fiction, yet all narrative fiction cannot be reduced merely to the dyad of an author and a narrator; both of these approaches are necessary though neither is sufficient to encompass the range of narrative fiction. 5) The notion of a career implied author is a useful one and deserves to be retained and further explored. 6) Within a work of fiction, the author can and often does speak directly to the reader. 7) Different communication levels are inherently permeable, and even in texts with a highly unreliable narrator, the levels can be collapsed and the author's voice can break through. 8) The category of the implied reader (or authorial audience) is likewise both more protean and more limited than is usually imagined and can contain more than one implied reader. 9) There are often fundamental asymmetries between the figures represented on the left and on the right sides of Chatman's diagram, that is, the production and reception of a narrative, and it should be superseded by more flexible and comprehensive figures.

Breaking through formalist barriers to include actual authors and readers can point the way to discuss other referential entities as well. We may well conclude with an observation made by Gogol in *Dead Souls*—of course I should properly say, the narrator of *Dead Souls,* but in this case I won't bother distinguishing them. In this passage, the speaker laments the deleterious effects of those who stupidly conflate fictional figures with actual persons, and I think we'll find his remarks apply equally well to actual authors and fictional narrators:

> In this house lived the closest and truest feminine friend of the lady who had just arrived. The author is very hard put to it to name both ladies in such a way as not to make them angry at him, as they used to be angry in the old days. To give them fictitious names is fraught with danger. No matter what name you think up, it will inevitably be found in some corner or other of our realm, for all it is so vast; someone is bound to hear it, and will inevitably become incensed. . . . But if one were to mention ranks—God save us, that would be still more dangerous! Nowadays

all our ranks and classes are in so touchy a mood that anything and everything which may be between the covers of a printed book already has the appearance of personal remarks for them—such, evidently, is the spirit in the air. It suffices merely to say that there is a stupid man in a certain town, and it is already a personal reflection: a gentleman of respectable appearance will suddenly pounce upon you and set up a shout: "Why, I, too, am a man, ergo, I, too, am stupid!"—in a word, he'll surmise in the wink of an eye just what you're up to. (226)

Conclusion

VOICING THE UNSPEAKABLE

chapter eight

In his "Introduction to the Structural Analysis of Narratives," Roland Barthes observes that standard conceptions "seem to consider narrator and characters as real—'living'—people (the unfailing power of this literary myth is well known), as though a narrative were originally determined at its referential level." He quickly adds that narrators and characters, however, "are essentially 'paper beings'" (1977, 111). This leads directly to the important conclusion that "the psychological person (of referential order) bears no relation to the linguistic person, the latter never defined by states of mind, intentions or traits of character but only by its coded place in discourse. It is this formal person that writers of today are trying to speak and such an attempt represents an important subversion" (114). One can no longer presume the existence of a real human or a human-like narrator standing behind and above the discourse; in many works, there is only the discourse itself. Barthes would not go on to develop this idea narratologically, but instead gave up the idea of an essentialist model of narrative in favor of the infinite and irreducible free play of signifiers in the writerly text.

Others, however, have taken up this challenge and attempted to describe these unnatural narrators and extreme acts of narration in a systematic manner. Jean Ricardou continued this kind of theoretical analysis, usually taking it much further than Barthes was prepared to go. Among current narrative theorists, the most prominent is Monika

Fludernik who, in her seminal account of "games with telling" (1996, 278–303), identifies a number of non- or transmimetic narrating situations, including those of contemporary narratives that are "no longer recuperable as the consciousness of a narrator figure because the juxtaposed material was too heterogenous either stylistically or thematically to warrant integration as part of a verisimilar stream of consciousness" (287). She would continue to extend this approach in her impressive 2001 article, "Old Wine in New Bottles?," explicitly arguing against Genette's postulation that any narrative text implies the existence of a speaker of that text. Marie-Laure Ryan (2001) also approaches this position, noting that "the narrator is a theoretical fiction, and that the human-like, pseudonatural narrator is only one of its many possible avatars" (152). This is the direction narrative theory must continue to move toward if it is to accurately circumscribe the narratives of our time.

We may now articulate a number of reasons that seem to impel authors to invent new forms of narration. A primary motive is modern novelists' continuing desire to "make it new." There is an impulse in the history of literature to take successful techniques and develop them further. In the introduction I delineated a number of trajectories that all moved further away from the basic first and third person categories available at the beginning of the twentieth century. After the signal achievements of Joyce and Proust, later writers would continue to extend existing paradigms and invent novel forms of representing consciousness in fiction. It is one of the great achievements of twentieth century literature, and I like to think of this book as an act of homage to this brilliant century of narrative innovation. This leads to two trajectories. One is where the play of the narration becomes a significant drama in its own right, as we have seen in the numerous texts that shift from one pronominal form to another; many employ third, second, or first plural voices only to end with a first person speaker that claims or concludes the narration at the end of the work (respectively, Robbe-Grillet's *Dans le labyrinthe,* Oates' "You," and Conrad's *Nigger of the 'Narcissus'*). The other road leads to the posthumanist narrators announced by Barthes. As Robert Pinget (1978) once warned his translator about one of his most anti-mimetic novels: "Don't bother too much about logic: everything in *Passacaille* is directed against it" (96).

Another reason, interestingly, has an obliquely mimetic source: it is often perceived that different aspects of human experience can be better or more appropriately depicted through new techniques. The most obvious of these is the consonance between the "we" form of narration and the representation of a close-knit group of individuals whose shared experiences lead to common ways of thinking. Multiperson narration likewise provides a more thorough picture of the multiple, distinct discourses that inform a group or a single individual consciousness; for many writers, the most effective way to produce a dialogical sensibility is to reenact it through an assemblage of disparate voices. Importantly, the breakdown of the notion of a stable self has been effective in unleashing a polyphony of discourses within an individual and a compelling image of the fragmented nature of the self, as we have seen throughout this book. Lying in a hospital bed, Fuentes' Artemio Cruz, who is depicted in alternating third, first, and second person sections, speculates: "I try to remember my reflection: face cut up by unsymmetrical facets of glass, the eye very near and very far from its mate: a face distributed among three shimmering mirrors" (5). The act of memory is here an emblem of the multiple modes of representing a divided subjectivity.

Finally, we may point to a growing impatience with the illusionistic rhetoric of conventional fiction. Henry James was famously appalled when he observed that Trollope, in the middle of a novel, "concedes to the reader that he and his trusting friend are only 'making believe.' He admits that the events he narrates have not really happened, and that he can give the narrative any turn the reader may like best. Such a betrayal of a sacred office seems to me, I confess, a terrible crime" (1972, 31–32). As the subsequent history of the novel would soon reveal, James was on the wrong side of this debate. After all, the events of a novel have not really happened and the author can give them any turn the reader may like best.

Naturally, modern writers were not the only ones to act on such knowledge. The history of literature is rife with examples of authors who were happy to point out, whether obliquely or flagrantly, the fictionality of their fictions. This counter tradition runs from ancient authors like Aristophanes and Lucian to Rabelais and Shakespeare and on to Fielding, Sterne, Diderot, Jean Paul, and Gogol. Even authors of works ostensibly grounded in realistic codes of representation often cannot resist an anti-illusionistic gesture: think of Don Quixote discussing the written account of his earlier adventures at the beginning of the second part of the work, and surmising that only an enchanter could know what transpired when no one else was present, or Cervantes' parody of the "found manuscript" gimmick. Proust likewise has his narrator aver, very late in his novel, that of all the characters only his beloved Françoise was real.

It should thus come as no surprise that the analysis in this book of extreme, unusual, and outrageous acts of narration, often associated with the practices of postmodernism, has repeatedly brought us back to unexpected precursors among the modernists. We have seen Conrad pioneer "we" narration and multiperson narration, and Jean Rhys deploy second person narration. The Joyce of *Ulysses* has also helped develop the interlocutor, the permeable narrator, and the incommensurate narrator decades before postmodernism is usually thought to have begun.[1] The practice of a third person narrator suddenly revealing him- or herself to be a mere character-narrator reconstructing the entire narration, described in detail in Chapter One, has an origin in the sudden admission of the narrator of Virginia Woolf's 1922 novel *Jacob's Room* that she is not omniscient or apart from the narrative world previously depicted in standard third person fashion; she is instead one human being trying to infer the thoughts of another: "This was in his face. Whether we know what was in his mind was another question" (1922, 94). Faulkner, after having produced a major modernist work that juxtaposes different perspectives and voices in *The Sound and the Fury* (1929), goes on to violate mimetic constraints in his next novel, *As I Lay Dying* (1930), which includes the narrated speech of the dead mother, Darl's preternatural knowledge of his sister's thoughts, and the unnatural focalization of the first passage of the novel which, though narrated by Darl in the present tense, is depicted from a visual perspective that he does not occupy: "Although I am fifteen feet ahead of him, anyone watching from the cottonhouse can see Jewel's frayed and broken straw hat a full head above my own" (1987, 3).

Altogether, there is a close connection between the daring though subtle practices of the modernists and the more obvious techniques of later postmodernists. A look back at another text by Woolf shows how she would transcend the humanist narrators she had earlier employed in *Mrs. Dalloway* and *To the Lighthouse*. The narrating situation in *The Waves* is both quite unusual and unprecedented in the history of fiction. The work is presented as a series of spoken monologues, complete with quotation marks and tags identifying the speakers (e.g., "Rhoda said"). However, most of the quoted words are clearly not those of the characters, but rather stylized, lyrical expressions of thoughts and emotions the characters experience. Thus, a small child's sensibility is represented in the following language: "My roots go down to the depths of the world, through earth dry with brick, and damp earth, through veins of lead and silver. I am all fibre. All tremors shake me, and the weight of the earth is pressed to my ribs" (12). This most curious kind of narration (we may call it "monologized thought") pushes at the possible boundaries of represented speech and emotion, as well as any stable concept of mimetic representation. It also extends to the point of annihilation the idea of reliable narration.[2] Here too Woolf anticipates some key developments of postmodern unreliability, which we examined at the end of Chapter Five.

The larger implications of the trajectory of recent literary practice should be clear: the extreme narrators and acts of narration in contemporary fiction have continued to move ever further beyond the established boundaries of realism, humanism, and conventional representation, and these new works pose severe problems for narratological models that are solely based on mimetic works. After the death of the conventional, humanist narrator, everything becomes possible—except theorizing narration in the earlier, conventional manner. J. M. Coetzee expresses this situation in the following terms:

> When you opt for a single point of view from inside a single character, you can be opting for psychological realism, a depiction of one person's inner consciousness. And the word I stress here is realism, psychological realism. And what is going on in *In the Heart of the Country* is that that kind of realism is being subverted because, you know, she kills her father, and her father comes back, and she kills him again, and the book goes on for a bit, and then he's there again. So it's a different kind of game, an anti-realistic kind of game. (Cited in Penner, 1989: 57)

The very language Coetzee uses to describe his divergence from the model of psychological realism suggests that his practice is not merely different, but consciously opposed to this poetics, and indeed that it may not be fully comprehensible except in reference to the mimetic strictures it so palpably violates. This is why I argue in this book not for a different poetics but for an additional one; that is, for an antimimetic poetics that supplements existing mimetic theories. Such a model will allow us to greatly expand the area covered by narrative theory, and will allow it to embrace a host of earlier nonmimetic literatures. And only in this way can we begin to do justice to the most effective imaginative achievements in narrative in our time.

The central thrust of this book can be encapsulated in a passage from Beckett. In *Worstward Ho* (1983), one of his final works, we encounter the following lines: "Whose words? Ask in vain. Or not in vain if say no knowing. No saying. No words for him whose words. Him? One. No words for one whose words. One? It. No words for it whose words. Better worse so" (20). We have in this section a miniature version of much of the drama of narrating that comprises *The Unnamable:* a voice that is inherently unknowable, irreducible to the apparent speaker, addressee, or the one being depicted. Again there is a play with pronouns as the third person is assayed and rejected in favor of the ambiguous form, "one," which in turn is rejected for the more dehumanized "it." Within this movement we see the progression away from fixed, mimetic representations of possible human speakers engaging in the transmission of a conventional or natural narrative to a radically different kind of narration that transgresses these foundations in favor of an original free play with voice, person, and perspective.

To conclude, I believe we will be most effective as narrative theorists if we reject models that, based on categories derived from linguistics or natural narrative, insist on firm distinctions, binary oppositions, fixed hierarchies, or impermeable categories. This is most importantly the case concerning what are still claimed to be the foundational oppositions, those between homo- and heterodiegesis, first and third person narration, and carefully separated figures of actual author, implied author, and narrator in Chatman's model of the narrative transaction. As we have seen on virtually every page of this study, numerous important narratives elude, problematize, or collapse these oppositions. Not only are the categories incomplete; the sensibility behind such a division of the practice of narration is misdirected. Chinese box type models should always be viewed with suspicion or rejected outright since they can never do justice to the playful, transgressive, and hybridizing tendencies of narrative fiction. Instead of dichotomous typologies, we need to employ the concept of a spectrum (even, at times, an ourouborean one) to describe what writers of fiction actually produce. A first person narrator may closely resemble a human being or it may differ in many ways; it may be contradictory, multiple, quasi-human, or little more than a mass of inconsistent discourse that cannot be reduced to a single narrative voice or position. More precisely, we will find a spectrum of positions ranging from the human to the antihuman, the unified to the fragmented, the consistent to the contradictory. The distance between an author, an implied author, and a narrator may likewise vary greatly from extreme divergence to virtual identity. Texts may conform to existing conventions, like that of the appropriate knowledge for first or third person narrators, or may extend, reform, violate, or otherwise flout the convention. While it may be true that it is necessary to start doing theory with the established practices of nonfictional, natural, and conventional narration, this is only the beginning. One must be prepared to go far beyond if one is to have any hope of effectively describing the practice of Conrad, Joyce, Woolf, Faulkner, and Nabokov, to say nothing of Beckett and the more radical innovators associated with the *nouveau roman,* magic realism, and postmodernism. Narrative fiction is dynamic, mutable, subversive, and, above all, dialectical in its perpetual reconfiguring of adjacent genres and established practices. In its more innovative forms, its convention is to alter convention, its essence is to elude a fixed essence, and its nature is to seek out the unnatural.

Bibliography of "We" Narratives

appendix

1. NARRATIVES ENTIRELY OR LARGELY IN THE "WE" FORM

Franz Kafka, "Josephina, die Sängerin, oder Das Volk der Mäuse," 1924

Ignazio Silone, *Fontemara,* 1930

William Faulkner, "A Rose for Emily," 1930, "That Evening Sun," 1931, "A Justice," 1931, "Divorce in Naples," 1931, "Death Drag," 1932, "That Will Be Fine," 1935, "Shingles for the Lord," 1943, "A Courtship," 1948

Raja Rao, *Kanthapura,* 1938

Richard Wright, *12 Million Black Voices,* 1941

Alain Robbe-Grillet, "The Way Back," 1954

Mauro Senesi, "The Giraffe," 1963

Michael Butor, "La Gare St. Lazare," 1964

Gabriele Wohmann, stories in *Gegenangriff,* 1971, and *Laendisches Fest,* 1975

Pierre Silvain, *Les Eoliennes,* 1971

Ayi Kwei Armah, *Two Thousand Seasons,* 1973

Arlette and Robert Brechon, *Les noces d'or,* 1974

Donald Barthelme, "We dropped in at the Stanhope . . . ," 1978, in *The Teachings of Don B.,* 1992

Julio Cortázar, "Queremos Tanto a Glenda," 1981

Mark Helprin, "North Lights" in *Ellis Island and Other Stories,* 1981

Edouard Glissant, *La Case du commandeur,* 1981

———. *Mahogany,* 1987

John Barth, *Sabbatical,* 1982

Joan Chase, *During the Reign of the Queen of Persia,* 1983

Nathalie Sarraute, *Tu ne t'aimes pas,* 1989

Jeffrey Eugenides, *The Virgin Suicides,* 1993

Zakes Mda, *Ways of Dying,* 1995
Patrick Chamoiseau, *L'Esclave vieil homme et le molosse,* 1997
Joyce Carol Oates, *Broke Heart Blues,* 1999
Jill McCorkle, "Billy Goats," 2001
Yiyun Lee, "Immortality" and "Persimmons," 2005

2. NARRATIVES SUBSTANTIALLY IN THE "WE" FORM

Joseph Conrad, *The Nigger of the 'Narcissus,'* 1899
Henri Barbusse, *Feu,* 1916
Mario Vargas Llosa, *Los Cachorros,* 1967
Edouard Glissant, *Malemort,* 1975
Louise Erdrich, *Tracks,* 1988
Hazard Adams, *Many Pretty Toys,* 1999

3. NARRATIVES WITH SIGNIFICANT SECTIONS IN THE "WE" FORM

Gustave Flaubert, beginning of *Madame Bovary,* 1857
Yevgeny Zamyatin, *We,* 1924
Victor Serge, *Naissance de notre force,* 1931
Gertrude Stein, *Everybody's Autobiography,* Chapter 4, "America," 1937
Albert Camus, *La Peste,* 1947
Samuel Beckett, *L'Innommable,* 1950
Vladimir Nabokov, *Speak Memory,* Chapter 15, 1951
Carlos Fuentes, "Alma Pura," 1964
Maurice Roche, *Compact,* 1966
Ngugi wa Thiong'o, *A Grain of Wheat,* 1967
Toni Morrison, *The Bluest Eye,* 1970
Julia Alvarez, *How the Garcia Girls Lost Their Accents,* 1991
Jean Echenois, *Nous trois,* 1992
Patrick Chamoiseau, *Texaco,* "The Noutéka of the Hills" (121–31), 1992

notes

NOTES TO CHAPTER 1

1. I am here using the translation and paraphrasing of Patrick O'Neill (76). See his very different critique of treating the narrator in anthropomorphic terms (76–82).

2. See William Nelles' article, "Beyond the Bird's Eye: Animal Focalization," for a perceptive overview of some of these techniques.

3. This thesis on the gendering of narrators in turn is further corroborated from a different angle by Daniel Punday's canny work on the implicitly embodied form of even the most austere narrators (2003: 149–84). For a stimulating account of the ideological maneuverings of female authors who employ male narrators, see Scott Simpkins' 1992 article on "narrative cross dressing" in Sand and Shelley.

4. I discuss these and similar cases in a forthcoming article on postmodern authors as fictional characters.

5. And as we will see in Chapter Five, even this relation can be skewed in unexpected ways.

6. Even those contemporary biographers or historians who "record" the thoughts of their protagonists are making educated guesses; unlike the novelist, they do not *know* what went on in their subject's mind.

7. For an earlier discussion of the "contamination" of the narrator's language by that of a character, see Stanzel 192–93.

8. For a different reading of the play of voice and narration in this work, see Margolin (1990), who affirms that "the voice tries to give life to a 'you' lying on his back in the dark by telling him his whole life story from beginning to end" (431).

9. For a theoretically informed account of Powell's practice, see Felber (1995, 156–61); Drabble's novel will be discussed below.

10. For a discussion of the narrative ethics of such a practice, see Phelan (2005).

11. The only work I am aware of that moves in the opposite direction is Gertrude Stein's *Autobiography of Alice B. Toklas* (1933), which concludes with the following admission: "About six weeks ago Gertrude Stein said, it does not look to me as if you were ever going to write that autobiography. You know what I am going to do. I am going to write it for you. . . . And she has and this is it" (252). Since this is a nonfictional work, issues of omniscience do not arise. In the end its effect is rather like that of Norman Mailer describing himself in the third person in *The Armies of the Night* (1968).

12. This passage is translated by and cited in Ann Jefferson (1980: 100); she provides a good introduction to many of the more famous and extreme forms of narration in the *nouveau roman.*

13. I am here building on Fludernik's excellent account (1994) in *Natural Narrative,* 224–36.

14. On the differences between French, German, and English usages and implications of this pronoun, see Fludernik (1996, 232–35). It might be noted that the English translation does not employ the pronoun "one" to translate "*man.*"

NOTES TO CHAPTER 2

1. For several other titles, see Fludernik's bibliography (1994); for additional items, see Schofield (1999).

2. See, however, Irene Kacandes, who considers many second person texts as works in "the apostrophic mode" (2001, 141–96).

3. For additional discussion of the shifting of pronouns in Butor, see Morrissette ("You" 13–18), Passias, van Rossum-Guyon (114–74), and Kacandes (157–62).

4. DelConte makes a comparable point, observing that this novel suggests "that in the eighties, free choice was illusory. Second-person narration exemplifies this cultural climate, for it manifests in narrative technique the notion that someone or something outside of yourself dictates your thoughts and actions" (205).

5. Carlos Fuentes' *La Muerta de Artemio Cruz* is the only text I know of to use the future tense for standard second person narration.

6. For a thorough discussion of gender and the reader(s) of this novel, see Teresa de Lauretis's excellent article, "Reading the (Post) Modern Text." In it she notes, for example, that the narrative's "you" does address a female reader for six pages, after which Calvino seems to need to reassure the male reader that the book is not losing sight of him (139–40).

7. Jonathan Holden similarly observes that "most poems that deploy the blurred-you are far more effective when delivered by the poet in person to a live audience" (54).

NOTES TO CHAPTER 3

1. In rare cases, such as Donald Barthelme's short text, "We dropped in at the Stanhope . . . ," the "we" speaker remains unidentified throughout, creating an

irreversible estrangement effect.

2. For an exhaustive account of these possibilities from the perspective of linguistics, see Margolin ("Telling" 116–19).

3. Even during this scene, however, there is a significant return to a collective consciousness that is signaled by the reversion to "we" form: the solidarity of the men reappears while they selflessly work to free Wait from his berth below deck (66–73).

4. There may even be an allegorical image of this preternatural narrator in the figure of the captain, who is said to be "one of those commanders who speak little, seem to hear nothing, look at no one—and know everything, hear every whisper, see every fleeting shadow of their ship's life" (125); his inexplicable omniscience is an apt analogue for the oscillating perspectives of the uncanny voice of the text.

5. Ian Watt identifies a single narrator, specifically, "a special kind of privileged narrator who functions as a collective voice (101). Others postulate two (or even more) narrators. Jakob Lothe identifies two main kinds of narrator, one homodiegetic, the "'narrator as character' (*I* as personal pronoun)"; the other heterodiegetic "*they* as personal pronoun" (97), and goes on to claim that these two basic narrating perspectives are repeatedly modified and fused; ultimately he identifies six types of narrating positions. Still others find the text's narration to be a mistake: Jeremy Hawthorn refers to the work's "technical confusions in the manipulations of narrative perspective and distance" (101) and Marvin Mudrick condemns Conrad's "gross violation of point of view" (72).

6. More helpful perspectives on Conrad's play with voice are offered by John Lester, who argues that Conrad's narrative technique is "more controlled and more inventive than he has generally been given credit for" (170) and Bruce Hendricksen, who states that the text "deconstructs the subject who narrates by juxtaposing a third-person narrative voice that refers to the crew as 'they' with a first person voice that says 'we'" (27).

7. She does, however, occasionally possess surprisingly detailed knowledge of situations she is unlikely to have encountered, as Paul Brians points out (39).

8. As Brians notes, she states that "there are only twenty-four houses in the village. This seems tiny indeed, until we realize she is counting the houses of Brahmins" (34).

9. For an analysis of Glissant's three "we" novels, see Celia Britton; on the relation between Glissant and Chamoiseau, see Dawn Fulton.

10. Thus, one Yukon Native begins the story of her life with a history of her nation, the histories of her mother and other close relatives, and the origin myth of her people. "She does not even get to her own birth until page 52 (and then it is buried in a long list of her brother and sisters arranged in birth order)" (174).

11. The fusion of recently deceased tribesmen in the collective living subject, as "they" merges with "we," deserves quotation: "They would sit in the snow outside the door, waiting until from longing we joined them. We would all be together on the journey then, our destination the village at the end of the road" (5).

12. "We" narratives continue to proliferate and gain recognition: two of the stories in Yiyun Li's prize-winning collection, *A Thousand Years of Good Prayers* (2005), are written in the first person plural.

13. Monika Fludernik has identified a number of other texts that alternate "we" and "I" narration; these include Mauro Senesi's "The Giraffe" (1963),

Gabriele Wohman's "Fahrplan" (1968), John Barth's *Sabbatical* (1982), and Jean Echenois' *Nous trois* (1992). Fludernik notes that in these cases the *we* text usually represents an extended first person narrative, for example, in rendering the experience of childhood or of rural life, "and it therefore includes the first-person narrator in a larger community of playmates or village folk" ("*Natural*" 224). See the appendix to this volume for still more titles of other recent "we" narratives.

14. Indeed, the most recent criticism and theory of "we" narrations often explicitly rejects the parameters of realism: Britton (136), Woller (346–48), Fulton (1113n3).

15. Genette simply asserts that "the collective witness as narrator" is an unremarkable variant of homodiegetic narration (1980, 245n).

NOTES TO CHAPTER 4

1. Two important partial exceptions to this practice are Franz K. Stanzel's *A Theory of Narrative,* which includes a fine discussion of alternating first and third person pronominal reference in, for example, novels written by a protagonist that at times refers to himself in the third person, such as *Henry Esmond* (99–110); and Hazard Adams, who points toward a more fluid model of the narrative transaction in "Critical Constitution of the Literary Text: The Example of *Ulysses.*" Genette also describes several interesting examples of alternating persons in *Narrative Discourse* (243–47), only to deny the importance of person as a category of narrative analysis.

2. Thus, the rational self speaks in the first person, and always depicts the id in the third person. Interestingly, the id keeps attempting to use the first person plural, a practice which the disgusted I strenuously resists.

3. The specific novels referred to here are Atwood's *The Edible Woman,* Drabble's *The Waterfall,* Laurence's *The Fire Dwellers.*

4. For a compelling overview of the book's narrative stances, see Suleiman, 44–49.

5. For a perspicacious account of the complexities of Barthes's position, some of which are necessarily slighted in my summary remarks, see Andrew Brown (123–25). In *Writing Degree Zero,* Barthes had affirmed that "'he' is a typical novelistic convention," while the "I" can take "its place beyond convention" (35).

6. See Cohn (*Distinction* 163–80) for a sound refutation of this farfetched notion.

7. The few times we encounter the woman expressing herself in the first person occur primarily when her nemesis discovers and reads her old journals and letters the better to manipulate her. That is, we read her first person accounts through his eyes.

8. For a more extended discussion of this pronominal strategy, see Ostrovsky, 76–78.

9. For additional discussion of how women and gays have used the second person and other uncommon pronominal forms to combat stereotyping and enhance potential reader identification, see Fludernik, "Persons."

10. Much subjunctive second person narration could be rewritten using "one" instead of "you" with little change in meaning, as the following sentence suggests, "To get there you follow/one follows Highway 58. . . ." This similarity may have led Wittig's translator to use the English word "you" to render the ubiquitous

"on" of *L'Opoponax.* Wittig's subsequent annoyance over this choice suggests an important difference between the two, a difference I suspect is rooted in divergent narrative persons.

NOTES TO CHAPTER 5

1. This is equally true of a third superficially similar type: in *La Chute,* the narrator Clamence appears to be telling a story to an offstage audient, partially repeating that person's replies and responding to his questions as they occur or are imagined ("You are in business, no doubt? In a way? Excellent response!" [8]).

2. For an excellent recent discussion of the catechistic form of "Ithaca," see Thwaites.

3. Senn, it should be noted, has no use for Hayman's arranger: "If you want to label this entity—it or him or why not her or them?—Narrator or arranger you are in good critical company, but you won't find these personifications here [in Senn's work]" (45).

4. As Monika Fludernik observes, one encounters narratological "difficulties at the end of the episode, which resists transformation [into conventional categories of narration] because the questions 'Womb? Weary?,' 'With,' 'When,' and 'Where' cannot be interpreted realistically or made to tally with the preceding description of Bloom's posture in his bed" ("Ithaca," 94–95).

5. The earliest example of this "interpretive" kind of denarration that I am familiar with occurs in the ninth canto of Camões' *The Lusiads,* in which the riotous adventures of Vasco da Gama's crew on the Island of the Blessed, after being described with brio, are then stated to be merely allegorical depictions of the men being ravished by honor.

6. In addition to compelling examples from Pynchon, Brooke-Rose, Sukenik, and others, McHale cites the actual erasing of events in Clarence Major's *Reflex and Bone Structure:* "It's Dale who stands there, mouth open, watching us. I erase him" (20, in McHale, 99).

7. It will be helpful to quote Robbe-Grillet's description of Beckett's use of this practice: "in Beckett, there is no lack of events, but these are constantly in the process of contesting themselves, jeopardizing themselves, destroying themselves, so that the same sentence may contain an observation and its immediate negation" (*New Novel,* 33; cited in Begam, 217).

8. The most thorough treatment of this general phenomenon can be found in Carla Locatelli's *Unwording the World,* which concentrates on Beckett's fiction after 1972. For useful discussions of textual negations in *Molloy,* see Dearlove (64–67), Hill (72–78), and Connor (56–63), who observes that "Time, and the present moments or states of which it is made up, is endlessly reimagined, so that the present moment not only repeats another moment belonging to the past, but reconstitutes that moment" (62).

9. Here I must disagree with Brian McHale, who asserts that "the 'erased' state of affairs still persists, if only as a kind of optical afterimage" (1987: 99). I believe the examples adduced here show instead that denarration effectively undoes the earlier assertions, rendering them as if they had not occurred, as is the case with other statements (false statements, typographical errors, lies) once we learn the actual state of affairs.

10. Cohn's paper ("Discordant") identifies other theorists, such as Susan S. Lanser, who earlier had identified comparable distinctions; for the most capacious model of unreliability (which includes six types), see Phelan (2005, 49–53).

11. I am here both drawing on and straying from Emma Kafalenos' ingenious narratological account of indeterminacy in postmodern fiction (1992).

12. H. Porter Abbott discusses this kind of narrational slippage from a different perspective in his chapter on Beckett in *Diary Fiction* (201–2).

13. The reading I will be offering tends to corroborate the critical position set forth by Andrew Kennedy; it is opposed to scholars like J. E. Dearlove who asserts, "Beneath the apparent and artificial diversity of traditional associations is the universal figure of a self coming into being via its self-perceptions, of a narrator creating himself through his own narration" (61). Such a stance ultimately begs the question "a self" and "his own" narration, positions Beckett resolutely undermines. For a more nuanced and compelling framing of this issue that suggests Beckett "expresses an openness to the possibility of an extralinguistic personal force" that is "quite compatible with The Unnamable's suspicion of the knowing voice" (54–55), see Porter Abbott (1996: 52–62 and passim). For a catalogue of statements in the trilogy relevant to this debate, see Rabinovitz (95–101).

14. On the posthumanist implications of Beckett's assault on the concept of personal identity, see Eric Levy (1980: 70 and passim) and Begam (17–25, 149–55).

15. There are of course still more possibilities, several of which have been set forth by Gary Adelman (2004), 67–75, esp. 73.

16. Eyal Amiran also agues for an ultimately unified position (116–22).

17. I do not, however, entirely agree with Begam's conclusion, that the space of the in-between "not only refuses to resolve itself into either of these two terms but renders impossible their very articulation" (156). This unresolved opposition of both terms remains; Beckett does not allow us to move beyond it via a Derridean notion of *écriture.*

NOTES TO CHAPTER 6

1. For an overview and bibliography of narration in drama, see my articles on the subject (the later of which is partially reproduced in this chapter).

2. It can also function as a generative narrator, as it does in cases of Cocteau and Benmussa described below.

3. For a deft analysis of the interplay of voice and text in this play, see Kristin Morrison's book on narration in the drama of Beckett and Pinter (214–18).

NOTES TO CHAPTER 7

1. For an excellent, nuanced critical summary of this debate, see Phelan (2005, 38–49).

2. This is the only one of several definitions still circulating that I will defend, or believe to be defensible. See Nünning for a thorough refutation of many of these conceptions.

3. It is also the case that Eliot's narrators present themselves as male; at one point, one refers to the act of stroking his moustache.

4. For a magisterial account of the multiple yet unknowable identity of the actual authors and redactors of *Beowulf,* see Nelles, who concludes that its historical author "is composed of at least seven flesh-and blood people, among whom the initial creator is by far the least concrete" ("Implied" 23).

5. Genette makes this statement after adducing the admittedly monovocal work of collaborators like the brothers Goncourt; he does not consider any of the more challenging cases I mention below.

6. As David Hawkes notes in his introduction, the final chapters seem to be written by "someone who was very familiar with [Tsao's] drafts and wanted a different ending" (18).

7. The reviewer for *The Nation* wrote, "One fancies Mr. James hypnotically persuaded to take his place in the circle between facetious Mr. [John Kendrick] Bangs and soulful Elizabeth Stuart Phelps, and caused to produce an excellent parody of himself, as if in spite of himself" (Bendixen, xxxvi).

8. Naturally, some individual voices do emerge; they do not perfectly blend together into a single implied author (for example, there is a pronounced shift in tone between the farcical first chapter and the much more serious, feminist-inflected second chapter).

9. I pursue this analysis further in my article, "Bad Joyce."

10. Or perhaps it is that all authors of Harlequin romances aspire to reproduce the tone and sensibility of same implied author.

11. This does not imply that there is any easy way to determine such a correspondence, only that one may bring external evidence (essays, journal entries, conversations with friends) to bear on this question in a way that is pointless concerning, say, geographical correspondences.

12. For a recent discussion of this issue, see Lanser, "(Im)plying" 156–59.

13. For an elaborate schema employing eleven different levels including the actual author, our notion of the historical author, the arranger, the narrator, etc., see Hazard Adams, "The Critical Constitution of the Literary Text" (90–110).

14. For another example of a clear distinction of a discontinuous historical author, implied author, and narratee, see Nelles' discussion of *Gulliver's Travels* (43–45).

15. See also pp. 25–44 and 192–206.

16. I develop this position at length in my article, "The Other Reader's Response."

17. The best account of the gender of reading remains Patrocinio Schweickart's foundational essay, "Reading Ourselves," in which she states: "Reader response cannot take refuge in the objectivity of the text, or even in the idea that a gender-neutral criticism is possible" (38–39).

18. See Aarseth (1997) for a nuanced discussion of this issue (162–67).

NOTES TO CHAPTER 8

1. For a discussion of the postmodernism of *Ulysses,* see my article, "The Genealogies of *Ulysses.*"

2. See Ferrer (1990, 65–96) for an extended discussion of the oddities of this kind of narration, which he tentatively calls prosopopaea.

works cited

Aarseth, Espen J. *Cybertext: Essays on Ergodic Literature.* Baltimore: Johns Hopkins University Press, 1997.

Abbott, H. Porter. *Beckett Writing Beckett: The Author in the Autograph.* Ithaca: Cornell University Press, 1996.

———. *Diary Fiction: Writing as Action.* Ithaca: Cornell University Press, 1984.

Acker, Kathy, "Humility." *The Seven Cardinal Virtues,* ed. Alison Fell. London: Serpent's Tail, 1990. 115–31.

Adams, Hazard. *Many Pretty Toys.* Buffalo: SUNY Press, 1999.

———. "Critical Constitution of the Literary Text: The Example of *Ulysses.*" *Antithetical Essays in Literary Criticism and Liberal Education.* Tallahassee: Florida State University Press, 1990. 90–110.

Adelman, Gary. *Naming the Unnamable.* Lewisburg: Bucknell University Press, 2004.

Aichinger, Ilse. "Spiegelgeschichte." *Der Gefesselte: Erzahlungen.* Frankfurt A.M.: S. Fischer Verlag, 1967.

Alldridge, J. C. *Ilse Aichinger.* Chester Springs, PA: Dufour Editions, Inc., 1969.

Amiran, Eyal. *Wandering and Home: Beckett's Metaphysical Narrative.* University Park: Pennsylvania State University Press, 1993.

Armah, Ayi Kwei. *Two Thousand Seasons.* London: Heinemann, 1973.

Bal, Mieke. *Narratology: Introduction to the Theory of Narrative.* Toronto: University of Toronto Press, 1985 (1980).

Barbusse, Henri. *Under Fire.* Trans. Robin Buss. New York: Penguin, 2003.

Barthelme, Donald. *The Teachings of Don B.* New York: Turtle Bay, 1992.

Barthes, Roland. *Image Music Text.* Trans. Stephen Heath. New York: Hill and Wang, 1977.

———. *Roland Barthes.* Trans. Richard Howard. New York: Hill and Wang, 1977.

———. *Writing Degree Zero and Elements of Semiology.* Trans. Annette Lavers and Colin Smith. Boston: Beacon Press, 1968.
Beckett, Samuel. *Collected Shorter Plays.* New York: Grove, 1984.
———. *Worstward Ho.* New York: Grove, 1983.
———. *Company.* New York: Grove, 1980.
———. *Stories and Texts for Nothing.* New York: Grove, 1967.
———. *Three Novels: Molloy, Malone Dies, The Unnamable.* New York: Grove, 1958.
Begam, Richard. *Samuel Beckett and the End of Modernity.* Stanford, CA: Stanford University Press, 1996.
Bendixen, Alfred. "Introduction: The Whole Story behind *The Whole Family.*" *The Whole Family* by William Dean Howells et al. New York: Ungar, 1986.
Bennett, Arnold. *The Old Wives' Tale.* New York: New American Library, 1963.
Ben-Zvi, Linda. *Samuel Beckett.* Boston: G. K. Hall, 1986.
Boehm, Beth. "Reeducating Readers: Creating Expectations for *The Golden Notebook.*" *Narrative* 5 (1997): 88–98.
Bonheim, Helmut. "Narration in the Second Person." *Recherches Anglaises et Americaines* 16 (1983): 69–80.
Booth, Wayne C. "Resurrection of the Implied Author: Why Bother?" *A Companion to Narrative Theory.* Ed. James Phelan and Peter Rabinowitz. Malden, MA: Blackwell, 2005. 75–88.
———. *The Rhetoric of Fiction.* 2nd ed. Chicago: University of Chicago Press, 1983 (1961).
Borges, Jorge Luis. *Collected Fictions.* Trans. Andrew Hurley. New York: Penguin, 1998.
Bouloumié, Arlette. "Writing and Modernism: Michel Tournier's *Friday.*" *Style* 26 (1992): 447–56.
Branigan, Edward. *Point of View in the Cinema.* Amsterdam: Mouton, 1984.
Brecht, Bertold. *Brecht on Theatre.* Trans. by John Willett. New York: Hill and Wang, 1964.
Brians, Paul. *Modern South Asian Literature in English.* Westport, CN: Greenwood Press, 2003.
Britton, Celia. "Collective Narrative Voice in Three Novels by Edouard Glissant." *An Introduction to Caribbean and Francophone Writing,* ed. Sam Haigh. Oxford: Berg, 1999. 135–47.
Brooke-Rose, Christine. *Thru.* London: Hamish Hamilton, 1975.
Brown, Andrew. *Roland Barthes: The Figures of Writing.* Oxford: Oxford University Press, 1992.
Butor, Michel. *Inventory.* Trans. Richard Howard. New York: Simon and Schuster, 1968.
———. *A Change of Heart.* Trans. Jean Stewart. New York: Simon and Schuster, 1959.
———. *La Modification.* Paris: Minuit, 1957.
Calvino, Italo. *Under the Jaguar Sun.* Trans. William Weaver. New York: Harcourt Brace, 1988.
———. *If on a winter's night a traveller.* Trans. William Weaver. New York: Harcourt Brace Jovanovich, 1981.
Carroll, David. "Introduction." *George Eliot: The Critical Heritage.* London: Routledge and Kegan Paul, 1971.

Chambers, Ross. *Facing It: AIDS Diaries and the Death of the Author.* Ann Arbor: University of Michigan Press, 1998.

Chase, Joan. *During the Reign of the Queen of Persia.* New York: Harper and Row, 1983.

Chatman, Seymour. *Story and Discourse: Narrative Structure in Fiction and Film.* Ithaca: Cornell University Press, 1978.

Cobham, Rhonda. "Misgendering the Nation: African Nationalist Fictions and Nuruddin Farah's *Maps*." *Nationalisms and Sexualities.* Ed. Andrew Parker et al. New York: Routledge, 1992. 42–59.

Cohn, Dorrit. "Discordant Narration." *Style* 34 (2000): 307–16.

———. *The Distinction of Fiction.* Baltimore: Johns Hopkins University Press, 1999.

———. *Transparent Minds: Narrative Modes for Presenting Consciousness in Fiction.* Princeton: Princeton University Press, 1978.

Collier, Gordon. "Apparent Feature-Anomalies in Subjectivized Third-Person Narration." *Recent Trends in Narratological Research* (GRAAT vol. 21). Ed. John Pier. Tours: University of Tours, 1999. 129–52.

Connor, Steven. *Samuel Beckett: Repetition, Theory and Text.* Oxford: Basil Blackwell, 1988.

Conrad, Joseph. *The Collected Letters of Joseph Conrad.* Ed. Frederick R. Karl and Laurence Davies. Cambridge: Cambridge University Press, 1983.

———. *Complete Works.* London: Doubleday, 1921.

Culler, Jonathan. "Omniscience." *Narrative* 12.1 (2004): 22–34.

Dearlove, J. E. *Accommodating the Chaos: Samuel Beckett's Nonrelational Art.* Durham: Duke University Press, 1982.

de Lauretis, Teresa. "Reading the (Post) Modern Text: *If on a winter's night a traveller.*" *Calvino Revisited.* Ed. Franco Ricci. Ottawa: Doverhouse Editions, Inc., 1989. 131–45.

DelConte, Matt. "Why *You* Can't Speak: Second Person Narration, Voice, and a New Model for Understanding Narrative." *Style* 37:2 (2003): 204–19.

Diamond, Elin. "Refusing the Romanticism of Identity: Narrative Interventions in Churchill, Benmusa, Duras." *Performing Feminisms: Feminist Critical Theory and Theatre,* ed. Sue-Ellen Case. Baltimore: Johns Hopkins University Press, 1984. 92–105.

Diderot, Denis. "This is not a Story." *The Penguin Book of French Short Stories,* ed. Edward Marielle. Harmondsworth, UK: Penguin, 1968.

Dostoevsky, Fyodor. *Great Short Works of Fyodor Dostoevsky.* Ed.Ronald Hingley. New York: Harper, 1968.

Drabble, Margaret. *The Waterfall.* New York: New American Library, 1986.

Ellison, Ralph. *Invisible Man.* New York: Random House, 1972 (1952).

Erdrich, Louise. *Tracks.* New York: Henry Holt, 1988.

Eugenides, Jeffrey. *The Virgin Suicides.* New York: Farrar, Straus and Giroux, 1993.

Farah, Nuruddin. *Maps.* New York: Random House, 1986.

Faulkner, William. *As I Lay Dying.* New York: Random, 1987.

———. *Light in August.* New York: Random, 1987.

———. *Collected Stories.* New York: Random, 1977.

Ferrer, Daniel. *Virginia Woolf and the Madness of Language.* Trans. Geoffrey Bennington and Rachel Bowlby. New York: Routledge, 1990.

Fielding, Henry. *The History of Tom Jones, a Foundling*. Ed. Martin C. Battestin. Middleton, CT: Wesleyan University Press, 1975.

Fludernik, Monika. "New Wine in Old Bottles?: Voice, Focalization, and New Writing." *New Literary History* 32 (2001): 619–38.

———. *Towards a 'Natural' Narratology*. London, New York: Routledge, 1996.

———. "Pronouns of Address and 'Odd' Third Person Forms: The Mechanics of Involvement in Fiction." *New Essays in Deixis*. Ed. Keith Green. Amsterdam: Rodopi, 1995. 99–129.

———. "Introduction: Second-Person Narrative and Related Issues." *Style* 28 (1994): 281–311.

———. "Second-Person Narrative: A Bibliography." *Style* 28 (1994): 525–48.

———. "'Ithaca'—An Essay in Non-Narrativity." *International Perspectives on James Joyce*. Ed. Gottlieb Gaiser. Troy, NY: Whitston, 1986. 90–107.

Foley, Barbara. *Telling the Truth: The Theory and Practice of Documentary Fiction*. Ithaca: Cornell University Press, 1989.

Ford, Ford Madox. *The Good Soldier*. Oxford: Oxford University Press, 1990.

Forster, E. M. *Aspects of the Novel*. New York: Harcourt, Brace, Jovanovich, n.d. (1927).

Frye, Joanne S. *Living Stories, Telling Lives: Women and the Novel in Contemporary Experience*. Ann Arbor: University of Michigan Press, 1986.

Fuentes, Carlos. *Obras Completas*. Vol. 1. Mexico City: Aguilar, 1974.

———. *Aura*. New York: Farrar, Straus and Giroux, 1965.

———. *The Death of Artemio Cruz*. Trans. Sam Hileman. New York: Farrar, Straus and Giroux, 1964.

Fugard, Athol. *My Children! My Africa!* New York: Theatre Communications Group, 1990.

Fulton, Dawn. "*Romans des Nous:* The First Person Plural and Collective Identity in Martinique." *The French Review* 76 (6), 2003: 1104–14.

Gallant, Mavis. "With a Capital T." *Home Truths*. New York: Random House, 1985. 317–30.

Genette, Gérard. *Narrative Discourse Revisited*. Trans. Jane E. Lewin. Ithaca: Cornell University Press, 1988 (1983).

———. *Narrative Discourse: An Essay in Method*. Trans. Jane E. Lewin. Ithaca: Cornell University Press, 1980 (1972).

Gissing, George. *New Grub Street*. New York: Modern Library, 2002.

Glissant, Edouard. *Caribbean Discourse: Selected Essays*. Trans. J. Michael Dash. Charlottesville: University of Virginia Press, 1989.

Gogol, Nikolai. *Dead Souls*. Trans. Bernard G. Guerney. New York: Modern Library, 1965.

Goytisolo, Juan. *Landscapes after the Battle*. Trans. Helen Lane. New York: Seaver Books, 1987 (1982).

Greene, Gayle. *Changing the Story: Feminist Fiction and the Tradition*. Bloomington: Indiana University Press, 1991.

Hampson, Robert. "'Allowing for Possible Error': Education and Catechism in 'Ithaca.'" *Joyce's "Ithaca,"* ed. Andrew Gibson. *European Joyce Studies* 6. Amsterdam: Rodopi, 1996. 229–67.

Hawkes, David. "Introduction." *The Story of the Stone,* Cao Xueqin. Trans. David Hawkes. Baltimore: Penguin, 1973. Volume 1, 15–45.

Hawkes, John. *The Lime Twig*. New York: New Directions, 1961.
———. *Virginie: Her Two Lives*. New York: Harper, 1982.
Hawthorn, Jeremy. *Joseph Conrad: Narrative Technique and Ideological Commitment*. London: Arnold, 1990.
Hayles, N. Katherine. *How We Became Posthuman: Virtual Bodies in Cybernetics, Literature, and Informatics*. Chicago: University of Chicago Press, 1999.
Hayman, David. *Ulysses: The Mechanics of Meaning*. Rev. Ed. Madison: University of Wisconsin Press, 1982.
Helprin, Mark. *Ellis Island and Other Stories*. New York: Harcourt, Brace, Jovanovich, 1981.
Hendricksen, Bruce. *Nomadic Voices: Conrad and the Subject of Narrative*. Urbana: University of Illinois Press, 1992.
Herman, David. *Story Logic: Problems and Possibilities of Narrative*. Lincoln: University of Nebraska Press, 2002.
Hesla, David H. *The Shape of Chaos: An Interpretation of the Art of Samuel Beckett*. Minneapolis: University of Minnesota Press, 1971.
Hill, Leslie. *Beckett's Fiction: In Different Words*. Cambridge: Cambridge University Press, 1990
Holden, Jonathan. *The Rhetoric of the Contemporary Lyric*. Bloomington: Indiana University Press, 1980.
Howells, William Dean et al. *The Whole Family: A Novel by Twelve Authors*. New York: Ungar, 1986.
Husson, Didier. "The Logic of Narrative Possibilities: A Study of the Compatibilities among the Variables of Narrative." *Poetique* 22 (1991): 289–313.
Hwang, David Henry. *M. Butterfly*. New York: NAL, 1989.
Irigaray, Luce. *The Irigaray Reader*. Ed. Margaret Whitford. Oxford: Basil Blackwell, 1991.
Jaffe, Audrey. *Vanishing Points: Dickens, Narrative, and Omniscience*. Berkeley: University of California Press, 1991.
James, Henry. *Theory of Fiction: Henry James*. Ed. James E. Miller, Jr. Lincoln: University of Nebraska Press, 1972.
Jefferson, Ann. *The Nouveau Roman and the Poetics of Fiction*. Cambridge: Cambridge University Press, 1980.
Joyce, James. *Ulysses: The Corrected Text*. Ed. Gabler et al. New York: Random, 1986.
Kacandes, Irene. *Talk Fiction: Literature and the Talk Explosion*. Lincoln: University of Nebraska Press, 2001.
Kafalenos, Emma. "Toward a Typology of Indeterminacy in Postmodern Narrative." *Comparative Literature* 44 (1992): 380–408.
Kayser, Wolfgang. *Entstehung und Krise des modernen Romans*. Stuttgart: Metzler, 1954.
Keen, Suzanne. *Narrative Form*. New York: St. Martin's, 2003.
Kennedy, Andrew K. *Samuel Beckett*. Cambridge: Cambridge University Press, 1989.
Kincaid, Jamaica. *A Small Place*. New York: Penguin, 1988.
Kingston, Maxine Hong. *The Woman Warrior: Memoir of a Girlhood among Ghosts*. New York: Knopf, 1977.
Kirby, John T. "Toward a Rhetoric of Poetics: Rhetor as Author and Narrator." *Journal of Narrative Technique* 22 (1992): 1–22.

Kozloff, Sarah. *Invisible Storytellers: Voice-Over Narration in American Fiction and Film.* Berkeley: University of California Press, 1988.

Lanser, Susan S. "(Im)plying the Author." *Narrative* 9 (2001): 153–60.

———. "Queering Narratology." *Ambiguous Discourse: Feminist Narratology and British Women Writers,* ed. Kathy Mezei. Chapel Hill: University of North Carolina Press, 1996. 250–61.

———. *Fictions of Authority: Women Writers and Narrative Voice.* Ithaca: Cornell University Press, 1992.

———. *The Narrative Act: Point of View in Prose Fiction.* Princeton: Princeton University Press, 1981.

Lawrence, Karen. *The Odyssey of Style in Ulysses.* Princeton: Princeton University Press, 1981.

Lejeune, Philippe. "The Autobiographical Contract." *French Literary Theory Today,* ed. Tzvetan Todorov. Cambridge: Cambridge University Press, 1982. 192–222.

Lester, John. "Conrad's Narrators in *The Nigger of the 'Narcissus.'*" *Conradiana* 12 (1980): 163–72.

Levy, Eric. *Beckett and the Voice of the Species.* Totowa, NJ: Barnes and Noble, 1980.

Lispector, Clarice. *The Stream of Life.* Trans. Elizabeth Lowe and Earl Fritz. Minneapolis: University of Minnesota Press, 1989.

Livingston, Paisley. *Art and Intention: A Philosophical Study.* Oxford: Oxford University Press, 2005.

Locatelli, Carla. *Unwording the World: Samuel Beckett's Prose Works after the Nobel Prize.* Philadelphia: University of Pennsylvania Press, 1990.

Lothe, Jakob. *Conrad's Narrative Method.* Oxford: Clarendon Press, 1989.

Macaskill, Brian. "Charting J. M. Coetzee's Middle Voice." *Contemporary Literature* 35 (1994): 441–75.

Margolin, Uri. "Collective Perspective, Individual Perspective, and the Speaker in Between: On 'We' Literary Narratives." *New Perspectives on Narrative Perspective,* ed. Willie van Peer and Seymour Chatman. Albany: SUNY Press, 2001. 241–55.

———. "Telling Our Story: On 'We' Literary Narratives." *Language and Literature* 5: 2 (1996): 115–33.

———. "Narrative 'You' Revisited." *Language and Style* 23: 4 (1990): 425–46.

Martin, Timothy. "*Ulysses* as a Whole." *A Collideorscape of Joyce,* ed. Ruth Frehner and Ursula Zeller. Dublin: Lilliput, 1998. 202–14.

Martin, Wallace. *Recent Theories of Narrative.* Ithaca: Cornell University Press, 1986.

McCarthy, Mary. *The Company She Keeps.* New York: Harcourt, Brace, 1942.

McHale, Brian. *Postmodernist Fiction.* New York: Methuen, 1987.

———. "'You Used to Know What These Words Mean': Misreading *Gravity's Rainbow.*" *Language and Style* 18 (1985): 93–118.

McInerney, Jay. *Bright Lights, Big City.* New York: Random House, 1984.

Mda, Zakes. *Ways of Dying.* New York: Farrar, Straus and Giroux, 1995.

Merwin, W. S. "The Second Person." *The Miner's Pale Children.* New York: Atheneum, 1970. 116–17.

Minh-Ha, Trinh T. *Woman, Native, Other: Writing Postcoloniality and Feminism.*

Bloomington: University of Indiana Press, 1989.
Moore, Lorrie. *Self-Help*. New York: NAL, 1986.
Moorjani, Angela K. *Abysmal Games in the Novels of Samuel Beckett*. North Carolina Studies in the Romance Languages and Literatures, Number 219. Chapel Hill: University of North Carolina at Chapel Hill, Department of Romance Languages, 1982.
Moravia, Alberto. *Two: A Phallic Novel*. Trans. Angus Davidson. New York: Farrar, Straus and Giroux, 1972.
Morris, Adalaide. "First Persons Plural in Contemporary Feminist Fiction." *Tulsa Studies in Women's Literature* 11 (1992): 11–29.
Morrison, Kristin. *Canters and Chronicles: The Use of Narrative in the Plays of Samuel Beckett and Harold Pinter*. Chicago: University of Chicago Press, 1983.
Morrissette, Bruce. *The Novels of Robbe-Grillet*. Ithaca: Cornell University Press, 1975.
———. "Narrative 'You' in Contemporary Literature." *Comparative Literature Studies* 2 (1965): 1–24.
Mudrick, Marvin. "The Artist's Conscience and *The Nigger of the 'Narcissus.'*" *Twentieth Century Interpretations of The Nigger of the 'Narcissus,'* ed. John A. Palmer. Englewood Cliffs, NJ: Prentice Hall, 1969.
Nabokov, Vladimir. *The Annotated Lolita*. Ed. Alfred Appel, Jr. New York: McGraw Hill, 1970.
Nelles, William. "Historical and Implied Authors and Readers." *Comparative Literature* 45 (1993): 22–46.
———. "Beyond the Bird's Eye: Animal Focalization." *Narrative* 9.2 (2001): 188–94.
———. "Omniscience for Atheists: Or, Jane Austen's Infallible Narrator." *Narrative* 14.2 (2006): 118–31.
Ngugi wa Thiong'o. *A Grain of Wheat*. London: Heinemann, 1967.
Nielsen, Henrik Skov. "The Impersonal Voice in First-Person Fiction." *Narrative* 12 (2004) 133–50.
Norris, Margot. *Suspicious Readings of Joyce's Dubliners*. Philadelphia: University of Pennsylvania Press, 2003.
Nünning, Ansgar. "Deconstructing and Reconceptualizing the Implied Author: The Resurrection of an Anthropomorphized Passepartout or the Obituary of a Critical Phantom?" *Grenzüberschreitungen: Narratologie im Kontext,* ed. Walter Grunzweig and Andreas Solbach. Tübingen: Günther Narr Verlag, 1999. 53–73.
Oates, Joyce Carol. *Broke Heart Blues*. New York: Dutton, 1999.
———. *The Wheel of Love and Other Stories*. New York: Vanguard, 1970.
O'Brien, Edna. *A Pagan Place*. London: Penguin, 1971 (1970).
O'Bryan-Knight, Jean. "From Spinster to Eunuch: William Faulkner's 'A Rose for Emily' and Mario Vargas Llosa's *Los cachorros*." *Comparative Literature Studies* 34 (1997): 328–47.
O'Neill, Patrick. *Fictions of Discourse: Reading Narrative Theory*. Toronto: University of Toronto Press, 1994.
Orieux, Jean. *Voltaire*. Trans. Barbara Bray and Helen R. Lane. Garden City, NY: Doubleday, 1979.

Ortiz-Robles, Mario. "George Eliot's Middle Voice." Paper read at the 19th Narrative Conference, Burlington, VT, April 24, 2004.

Ostrovsky, Erika. *A Constant Journey: The Fiction of Monique Wittig*. Carbondale: Southern Illinois University Press, 1991.

Passias, Katherine. "Deep and Surface Structure of the Narrative Pronoun *Vous* in Butor's *La Modification* and Its Relationship to Free Indirect Style." *Language and Style* 9 (1976): 197–212.

Peake, C. H. *James Joyce: The Citizen and the Artist*. Stanford, CA: Stanford University Press, 1977.

Penner, Dick. *Countries of the Mind: The Fiction of J. M. Coetzee*. Westport, CT: Greenwood, 1989.

Perec, Georges. *Un homme qui dort*. Paris: Denoel, 1967.

Phelan, James. *Living to Tell about It: A Rhetoric and Ethics of Character Narration*. Ithaca: Cornell University Press, 2005.

———. "Narrative Judgments and the Rhetorical Theory of Narrative: Ian McEwan's *Atonement*." *A Companion to Narrative Theory*, ed. James Phelan and Peter Rabinowitz. Malden, MA: Blackwell, 2005. 322–36.

———. "*Self-Help* for Narratee and Narrative Audience: How 'I'—and 'You'?—Read 'How.'" *Style* 28 (1994): 350–65.

———. *Reading People, Reading Plots: Character, Progression and the Interpretation of Narrative*. Chicago: University of Chicago Press, 1989.

Phillips, Caryl. *Crossing the River*. New York: Knopf, 1994.

Pinget, Robert. *Passacaglia*. Trans. Barbara Wright. New York: Red Dust, 1978.

Prince, Gerald. *A Dictionary of Narratology*. Rev. ed. Lincoln: University of Nebraska Press, 2003.

———. "The Disnarrated." *Style* 22 (1988): 1–8.

Proust, Marcel. *Marcel Proust on Art and Literature*. Trans. Sylvia Townsend Warner. New York: Carroll and Graf, 1984.

Punday, Daniel. *Narrative Bodies: Toward a Corporeal Narratology*. New York: Palgrave Macmillan, 2003.

Queenan, Joe. "Ghosts in the Machine." *New York Times Book Review*. March 20, 2005. 7–8.

Rabinovitz, Rubin. *Innovation in Samuel Beckett's Fiction*. Urbana: University of Illinois Press, 1992.

Rabinowitz, Peter. "'Betraying the Sender': The Rhetoric and Ethics of Fragile Texts." *Narrative* 2 (1994): 301–13.

Rao, Raja. *Kanthapura*. New York: New Directions, 1963.

Richardson, Brian. "Bad Joyce: Anti-Aesthetic Practices in *Ulysses*." *Hypermedia Joyce Studies* 7.1 (2006). http://www.hjs.ff.cuni.cz; http://www.geocities.com/hypermedia_joyce/.

———. "When the Author Is the Narrator: Nabokov's Textual Intrusions and the Question of Fictionality" (forthcoming).

———. "Introduction: Conrad and the Reader." *Conradiana* 35 (2003): 1–6.

———. "Voice and Narration in Postmodern Drama." *New Literary History* 32 (2001): 681–94.

———. "The Genealogies of *Ulysses*, the Invention of Postmodernism, and the Narratives of Literary History." *ELH* 67 (2000): 1035–54.

———. "Linearity and Its Discontents: Rethinking Narrative Form and Ideological

Valence." *College English* 62 (2000): 685–95.
———. "The Other Reader's Response: On Multiple, Divided, and Oppositional Audiences." *Criticism* 39 (1997): 31–53.
———. "Point of View in Drama: Diegetic Monologue, Unreliable Narrators, and the Author's Voice on Stage." *Comparative Drama* 22 (1988): 193–214.
Rimmon-Kenan, Shlomith. *Narrative Fiction: Contemporary Poetics.* London: Methuen, 1983.
Robbe-Grillet, Alain. *Project for a Revolution in New York.* Trans. Richard Howard. New York: Grove, 1972.
———. *For a New Novel: Essays on Fiction.* Trans. Richard Howard. New York: Grove, 1965.
———. *Two Novels by Robbe-Grillet: Jealousy and In the Labyrinth.* Trans. Richard Howard. New York: Grove, 1965.
Roche, Maurice. *Compact.* Trans. Mark Pollizotti. Elmwood Park, IL: Dalkey Archive, 1988.
———. *Compact.* Paris: Seuil, 1966.
Rushdie, Salman. *Midnight's Children.* New York: Knopf, 1981.
Ryan, Marie-Laure. "The Narratorial Functions: Breaking Down a Theoretical Primitive." *Narrative* 9 (2001): 146–52.
Sarraute, Nathalie. *You Don't Love Yourself.* Trans. Barbara Wright. New York: Brazilier, 1990.
———. *Tu ne t'aimes pas.* Paris: Gallimard, 1989.
Schofield, Dennis. *Second Person Fiction.* http://members.westnet.com.au/emmas/2p/index2.htm (accessed 1999).
Schweickart, Patrocinio P. "Reading Ourselves: Toward a Feminist Theory of Reading." *Gender and Reading: Essays on Readers, Texts, and Contexts.* Ed. Elizabeth A. Flynn and Patrocinio P. Schweickart. Baltimore: Johns Hopkins University Press, 1986. 31–62.
Senn, Fritz. "'Ithaca': Portrait of the Chapter as a Long List." *Joyce's "Ithaca,"* ed. Andrew Gibson. Amsterdam: Rodopi, 1996. 31–76.
Serge, Victor. *Birth of our Power.* Trans. Richard Greeman. New York: Doubleday, 1967.
Silone, Ignazio. *The Abruzzo Trilogy: Fontamara, Bread and Wine, The Seed Beneath the Snow.* Trans. Eric Mosbacher. South Royalton, VT: Steerforth Italia, 2000.
Simion, Eugen. *The Return of the Author.* Evanston, IL: Northwestern University Press, 1996.
Simpkins, Scott. "They Do the Men in Different Voices: Narrative Cross Dressing in Sand and Shelley." *Style* 26 (1992): 400–418.
Sollers, Philippe. *Event.* Trans. Bruce Benderson and Usule Molinaro. New York: Red Dust, 1986.
Stanzel, Franz K. *A Theory of Narrative.* Trans. Charlotte Goedsche. Cambridge: Cambridge University Press, 1984 (1979).
Stoppard, Tom. *Squaring the Circle: Poland 1980–81.* London: Faber and Faber, 1984.
Suleiman, Susan R. "Of Readers and Narratees: The Experience of *Pamela.*" *L'Esprit Createur* 21 (1981): 89–97.
Thackeray, William Makepeace. *Vanity Fair. The Works of William Makepeace*

Thackeray. The Biographical Edition. New York: Harpers, 1903. Vol. 1.

Thwaites, Tony. "Catechistics, or Where was Moses When the Lights Went Out? Q, A, and Hospitality in 'Ithaca.'" *James Joyce Quarterly* (forthcoming).

Toolan, Michael J. *Narrative: A Critical Linguistic Introduction.* New York: Routledge, 1988.

van Rossum-Guyon, Francoise. *Critique du roman: Essai sur* La Modification *de Michel Butor.* Paris: Gallimard, 1970.

Vargas Llosa, Mario. *Los jefes, Los cachorros.* Barcelona: Seix Barral, 1991.

———. *The Cubs and Other Stories.* Trans. Gregory Kolovakos and Ronald Christ. New York: Noonday, 1989.

Vogel, Paula. *The Baltimore Waltz and Other Plays.* New York: Theatre Communications Group, 1996.

Vonnegut, Kurt. *Slaughterhouse-Five.* New York: Random, 1991 (1969).

Warhol, Robyn. "Making 'Gay' and 'Lesbian' into Household Words: How Serial Form Works in Armistead Maupin's *Tales of the City.*" *Contemporary Literature* 40 (1999): 379–402.

Warhol, Robyn R. *Gendered Interventions: Narrative Discourse in the Victorian Novel.* New Brunswick: Rutgers University Press, 1989.

Watt, Ian. *Conrad in the Nineteenth Century.* Berkeley: University of California Press, 1979.

Weldon, Fay. *The Cloning of Joanna May.* New York: Viking, 1990.

Williams, Tennessee. *The Glass Menagerie.* New York: New Directions, 1970.

Willis, Sharon. *Marguerite Duras: Writing on the Body.* Urbana: University of Illinois Press, 1987.

Wilson, George M. *Narration in Light: Studies in Cinematic Point of View.* Baltimore: Johns Hopkins University Press, 1986.

Woller, Joel. "First-person Plural: The Voice of the Masses in Farm Security Administration Documentary." *JNT: Journal of Narrative Theory* 29.3 (1999): 340–66.

Wong, Hertha D. Sweet. "First Person Plural: Subjectivity and Community in Native American Women's Autobiography." In *Women, Autobiography, Theory: A Reader.* Ed. Sidonie Smith and Julia Watson. Madison: University of Wisconsin Press, 1998. 168–78.

Woolf, Virginia. *The Diary of Virginia Woolf* (5 Volumes). Ed. Anne Olivier Bell. London: Penguin, 1977–84.

———. *The Waves.* New York: HBJ, n.d. (1931).

———. *A Room of One's Own.* New York: HBJ, n.d. (1929).

———. *To the Lighthouse.* New York: HBJ, n.d. (1927).

———. *Jacob's Room.* New York: HBJ, n.d. (1922).

Wright, Richard. *12 Million Black Voices.* New York: Thunder's Mouth, 1988.

Zamyatin, Yevgeny. *We.* Trans. Mirra Ginsburg, New York: Viking, 1972.

index

THEORY AND INTERPRETATION OF NARRATIVE
James Phelan and Peter J. Rabinowitz, Series Editors

Because the series editors believe that the most significant work in narrative studies today contributes both to our knowledge of specific narratives and to our understanding of narrative in general, studies in the series typically offer interpretations of individual narratives and address significant theoretical issues underlying those interpretations. The series does not privilege one critical perspective but is open to work from any strong theoretical position.

Narrative Causalities
Emma Kafalenos

Why We Read Fiction: Theory of Mind and the Novel
Lisa Zunshine

I Know That You Know That I Know: Narrating Subjects from Moll Flanders *to* Marnie
George Butte

Bloodscripts: Writing the Violent Subject
Elana Gomel

Surprised by Shame: Dostoevsky's Liars and Narrative Exposure
Deborah A. Martinsen

Having a Good Cry: Effeminate Feelings and Pop-Culture Forms
Robyn R. Warhol

Politics, Persuasion, and Pragmatism: A Rhetoric of Feminist Utopian Fiction
Ellen Peel

Telling Tales: Gender and Narrative Form in Victorian Literature and Culture
Elizabeth Langland

Narrative Dynamics: Essays on Time, Plot, Closure, and Frames
Edited by Brian Richardson

Breaking the Frame: Metalepsis and the Construction of the Subject
Debra Malina

Invisible Author: Last Essays
Christine Brooke-Rose

Ordinary Pleasures: Couples, Conversation, and Comedy
Kay Young

Narratologies: New Perspectives on Narrative Analysis
Edited by David Herman

Before Reading: Narrative Conventions and the Politics of Interpretation
Peter J. Rabinowitz

Matters of Fact: Reading Nonfiction over the Edge
Daniel W. Lehman

The Progress of Romance: Literary Historiography and the Gothic Novel
David H. Richter

A Glance Beyond Doubt: Narration, Representation, Subjectivity
Shlomith Rimmon-Kenan

Narrative as Rhetoric: Technique, Audiences, Ethics, Ideology
James Phelan

Misreading Jane Eyre: *A Postformalist Paradigm*
Jerome Beaty

Psychological Politics of the American Dream: The Commodification of Subjectivity in Twentieth-Century American Literature
Lois Tyson

Understanding Narrative
Edited by James Phelan and Peter J. Rabinowitz

Framing Anna Karenina: Tolstoy, the Woman Question, and the Victorian Novel
Amy Mandelker